Black Film Through a Psychodynamic Lens

Black Film Through a Psychodynamic Lens delves into the nuanced character development and narrative themes within the struggles and successes presented in Black films over the last five decades.

In this pioneering book, Katherine Marshall Woods looks at Black cinema from a psychological and psychoanalytic perspective. Focusing on a decade at a time, she charts the development of representation and creative output from the 1980s to the present day. She deftly moves from analyzing depictions of poverty and triumphs to highlighting the importance of cinema in shaping cultural identity while considering racial prejudice and discrimination. Adopting theoretical viewpoints from Freud to bell hooks, Marshall Woods examines the damaging effect on cultural psychology as a result of stereotypical racial tropes, and expertly demonstrates the healing that can be found when one sees oneself represented in an honest light in popular art.

From *Do the Right Thing, The Color Purple*, and *Malcolm X* to contemporary classics like *12 Years a Slave, Black Panther*, and *American Fiction*, this book is an essential read for those interested in the intersection between Psychology, Psychoanalysis, Film Theory, and African American cultural identity.

Katherine Marshall Woods is a media and licensed clinical psychologist based in Washington, DC and an assistant professor at the George Washington University, USA.

"In *Black Film Through a Psychological Lens*, Dr. Marshall Woods offers a powerful explanatory framework for films from the early 20th century until today, moving from discussion of painful stereotypes especially prevalent in early films, to depictions of narratives of resilience, posttraumatic growth, creativity, and empowerment reflecting the broad range of Black Lives today. The author ably utilizes an insightful culturally nuanced and modern psychodynamic analytic framework, particularly with regard to how defense mechanisms such as sublimation and reaction formation serve to illuminate how and why filmmakers create the films they do, and how and why viewers respond in the ways they do. Marshall Woods is to be commended for providing insights into both the better known, as well as into some less familiar, Black films from the early years through the first quarter of the 21st century."

Grant J. Rich, *PhD, President Society for Media Psychology and Technology, Walden University*

"Dr. Katherine Marshall Woods' '*Black Film Through a Psychodynamic Lens*' is a seminal work that meticulously dissects the psychological motifs embedded within Black cinema alongside pertinent psychological research, highlighting the complexities of race, identity, and culture in film. Through insightful chapter divisions, each dedicated to a specific era of filmmaking, Dr. Marshall Woods adeptly synthesizes the synopses of pivotal films with insightful analyses of the profound psychological themes relevant to the Black community. This book is vital in fostering inclusivity within film anthology, highlighting the underappreciated significance of Black cinema, its psychological influence and its indispensable role in shaping broader cinematic discourse on American life. A compelling must-read for scholars, practitioners, and film enthusiasts alike."

Dr. Tamika Damond, Founder of Believe Psychology Film Festival

Black Film Through a Psychodynamic Lens

Katherine Marshall Woods

LONDON AND NEW YORK

Designed cover image: ©Getty

First published 2025
by Routledge
4 Park Square, Milton Park, Abingdon, Oxon OX14 4RN

and by Routledge
605 Third Avenue, New York, NY 10158

Routledge is an imprint of the Taylor & Francis Group, an informa business

© 2025 Katherine Marshall Woods

The right of Katherine Marshall Woods to be identified as author of this work has been asserted in accordance with sections 77 and 78 of the Copyright, Designs and Patents Act 1988.

All rights reserved. No part of this book may be reprinted or reproduced or utilised in any form or by any electronic, mechanical, or other means, now known or hereafter invented, including photocopying and recording, or in any information storage or retrieval system, without permission in writing from the publishers.

Trademark notice: Product or corporate names may be trademarks or registered trademarks, and are used only for identification and explanation without intent to infringe.

British Library Cataloguing-in-Publication Data
A catalogue record for this book is available from the British Library

ISBN: 9781032508412 (hbk)
ISBN: 9781032508399 (pbk)
ISBN: 9781003399902 (ebk)

DOI: 10.4324/9781003399902

Typeset in Times New Roman
by codeMantra

To know that my people played on this playground
during film's inception and through the course of its
development persisted and thrived, acknowledges
that our contribution has been both meaningful and
great. Albeit limited at times, it does not minimize the
significance Black film presence has had to our heritage,
to our culture, and to our nation and beyond.

Contents

Introduction   1
In the Beginning 2
Learning with Film 3
A Psychological Connection 5
Open to All 6
Disclaimer 6

1   Ease on Down the Road?   8
Motion Pictures' Influence 10
   The Price of Hollywood 11
   Gathering the Golden Bricks 15
   Creating Space, Race Films 15
   George and Noble Johnson's Lincoln Motion Pictures
     Company 16
   Oscar Micheaux (1884–1951) 16
   Paving the Way 17
Black Film Through a Psychodynamic Lens 18
   Our Legacy 19

2   Living Black (1980–1989)   20
A Soldier's Story (1984) 21
Purple Rain (1984) 22
Krush Groove (1985) 24
She's Gotta Have It (1986) 25
Hollywood Shuffle (1987) 27
The Color Purple (1988) 28
Colors (1988) 30
Coming to America (1988) 31
Do the Right Thing (1989) 32

viii Contents

Harlem Nights (1989) 34
Legacy Films 36
  School Daze (1988) 36
  Glory (1989) 39
  Lean on Me (1989) 40
  Tap (1989) 42

3   Death and Rebirth to Evolution (1990–1999)   44

Trauma 45
  Including Boyz N the Hood (1991), Juice (1992), Poetic
    Justice (1993), Menace II Society (1993), Above the Rim
    (1994), Jason's Lyric (1994), Clockers (1995), Dead
    Presidents (1995), and Set It Off (1996) 45
Family 54
  Including The Best Man (1991), The Five Heartbeats (1991),
    Waiting to Exhale (1995), The Preacher's Wife (1996), Soul
    Food (1997), Life (1999), and The Wood (1999) 54
Loving Passionately 57
  Mo' Better Blues (1990) 57
  Boomerang (1992) 58
  Higher Learning (1995) 60
  Love Jones (1997) 61
  How Stella Got Her Groove Back (1998) 62
Legacy Films 63
  Malcolm X (1992) 64
  What's Love Got to Do With It (1993) 65

4   Dreams Come True (2000–2009)   67

Love and Basketball (2000) 69
Drumline (2002) 70
Hustle and Flow (2005) 72
Dreamgirls (2006) 73
Stomp the Yard (2007) 75
Legacy Films 76
  Antwone Fisher (2002) 76
  Ray (2004) 78
  The Great Debaters (2007) 79

5   Unchained… Freedom (2010–2019)   81

Fences (2016) 82
Moonlight (2016) 82

Contents ix

Get Out (2017) 82
Black Panther (2018) 84
If Beale Street Could Talk (2018) 85
Sorry to Bother You (2018) 87
Queen and Slim (2019) 89
Legacy Films 90
  12 Years a Slave (2012) 90
  Selma (2014) 93
  Hidden Figures (2016) 95
  Detroit (2017) 95
  Marshall (2017) 96

6 Awaiting with Baited Breath (2020 and Beyond)   99
Da 5 Bloods (2020) 100
The Photograph (2020) 101
The Woman King (2022) 102
American Fiction (2023) 104
Legacy Films 106
  Judas and the Black Messiah (2021) 106
  King Richard (2021) 108
  Respect (2021) 109
  Till (2022) 111

Final Thoughts   113
The Yellow Brick Road to Hollywood 116

Special Thanks   *119*
Bibliography   *120*
Index   *129*

Introduction

When I became interested in the intersection of psychology and film, my childhood friend shared with me her lack of surprise. She reminded me of my teenage years spending Friday evenings at the closest movie theater to screen the latest movie featuring African American actors by Black filmmakers. She also recalled me convincing her to have conversations about said films on Monday when we returned to school. We talked about the themes, plots, characters, and the similarities and differences between films. During these talks we considered the feelings that accompanied being a member of the audience when viewing the film. Within those same years, despite being an art student, I knew that psychology would be the profession that I would embrace. I wanted to listen and provide a haven for individuals to discover who they were and work to make lifelong change. However, within the decades that followed, I became interested in sharing with others outside of the psychological community about the field using film as a vehicle to have discussions about psychological theories.

As responsibilities increased, creative time (outside of clinical creativity) decreased. It was not until I attended a holiday party that a colleague, soon to become my mentor and dear friend, asked, "What do you really want to be doing?" In that moment, I became acutely sensitive to the situation at hand. I realized that within that present minute was "a moment" happening. I needed to make a choice: provide the stock answer that reflected what I was doing with my career at the time, or share a dream that seemed unlikely to become a reality. When I responded that I would like to have a career using film to highlight the psychodynamic theories found within scripts, work with screenwriters and filmmakers consulting on their work to assist with psychological accuracy and enrich the characters in their films to better reflect the human condition, and, if possible, have conversations with the general public about psychodynamic theories in a friendly, digestible way using these films, it felt fantastical. Today, I am grateful I shared. It is due to a combination of his curiosity, care, and guidance in concert with my response and interest that this book is possible. With an honest answer provided in a colleague's living area, years of writing on this passion has yielded countless opportunities to share with the general public and fellow colleagues how an artistic expression created within films captures numerous psychodynamic

DOI: 10.4324/9781003399902-1

2 Introduction

theories in an artful way. With this commitment, the goal remains that the general public becomes familiar with psychological and psychodynamic findings in a non-threatening manner, that facilitates self-discovery and healing while contributing to the reduction of stigma within the area of mental health. And, what better way to do so than by engaging in a medium that has an infinite public reach to expose individuals to the breadth of human experiences, such as film?

In the Beginning

It was only less than a decade after the first film was created that the field of psychology became curious regarding the influence moving images would have upon individuals and culture. During this time, there was an understanding that cinema viewing was a psychological experience. The marital vows of psychology and film occurred in 1916 when a psychology professor from Harvard, Hugo Münsterberg, published *The Photoplay: A Psychological Study* (Cohen, 2002; Tan, 2018). This pioneering book created interest in the intersection of film and psychology, and was followed, fifteen years later, when a French psychologist, Lionel Laudry, published an article on the psychology of cinema, specifically examining the impact of music influences on the art (Cohen, 2002). Since then, the contribution of psychology in cinema has continued to grow; yet slowly.

It wasn't until the 1970s that psychology and film was embraced as a subdiscipline of academic psychology and gained traction (Tan, 2018). We have learned a great deal since. We consider the use of cinematography to present "a series of shots edited together to make a coherent visual story" (Germeys & Géry d'Ydewalle, 2007, p. 458). Film is the culmination of a complex collaboration among a variety of artists, and screening the film exposes one to the art of creative writing, cinematography, sound engineering, music composing, and more, creating "a successful work [that] requires harmony among them so that a coherent image emerges" (Cupchik, 2001, p. 72). From a psychological perspective, this coherent image does not transpire in the absence of intention. Rather, "filmmakers utilize cinematic techniques in creative ways to craft an evocative experience to best engage audiences" (Marshall Woods, 2024, p. 132). For example, "the appropriate application of music in film reflects psychological rules" (Cohen, 2005, p. 16) where tempos and tones are taken into consideration to conjure specific feelings within the film patron (Cohen, 2005; Martin, 2019). According to Cohen (2005), "Melodies in the major mode add to the level of happiness", "melodies in the minor mode decrease it" in turn (p. 21) and "music is specifically chosen or composed to complement the narrative and it is spotted in only at specific points in the drama" (p. 28). Further, "some types of music are designed to be unpleasant, be perceived negatively, and to create tension", which can be found within horror films respectively (Martin, 2019, p. 5). Martin (2019) continues that one "of the most successful, and the most common, auditory tropes in horror is the use of a loud sound after a prolonged period of silence—the so called jump scare" (p. 5).

As film is able to surface feelings within us, it equally has been able to influence our behavior. Specifically, films have been found to provide a short-term jolt in our

Introduction 3

"motivation to act" on situations we view within the film as problematic for ourselves (such as climate change concerns) and can "increase concern" in us in similarly short durations (Howell, 2011, p. 177). These findings have led us to be cognizant that "most viewers do not just consume the images and storylines in media and walk away untouched" (Eschholz et al., 2002, p. 301). Rather, "films are expected to form beliefs, influence opinions and change attitudes" (Kubrak, 2020, p. 2). "A single well-chosen feature film may contain a range of fertile issues" (Bluestone, 2000, p. 142) that can create personal discovery, growth, and healing. With this understanding, cinema can be a catalyst of individual and social evolution (Kashani, 2015).

In particular, over the last few decades, there have been beautiful, visible transitions noticed in how Americans engage with stigma in relation to mental health. Currently, and differently than in decades past, mental health stigma is being addressed directly by the public. Fostering mental health wellness and seeking psychiatric services is an act that is better accepted, where people are applauded for their bravery in seeking treatment. Historically, seeking services to assist with healthy mental wellbeing was often discouraged, mocked, and encouraged to be hidden from others. Regretfully, for some, this stance continues to perpetuate within the social fabrics of communities today. Therefore, acknowledging that not all persons and communities benefit the same from mental health services seems important. For instance:

> stigma and judgment prevent Black and African American people from seeking treatment for their mental illnesses. Research indicates that Blacks and African Americans believe that mild depression or anxiety would be considered 'crazy' in their social circles. Furthermore, many believe that discussions about mental illness would not be appropriate even among family.
>
> (Mental Health America, 2023)

The etiology and perpetuation of stigma within the African American community pertaining to mental health awareness, diagnosis, and treatment is a complex living construct that has complicated, well-entrenched roots that cannot be adequately addressed within this text. Yet, because there is an awareness that the stability of stigma has sustained a life within America amongst the African American community pertaining to mental health wellness, exploring how alternative mechanisms can work to help people become curious regarding psychology can be globally beneficial.

Learning with Film

Film has captivated audiences with compelling narratives; and, as a result, it has been actively used as a mechanism to provide a safe way to explore life's dynamics and events. According to Currie (2004), the faculties we use "making sense of film are, to a significant degree, those that we deploy in the project of making sense of the real world" (p. 106). Through motion pictures that depict fiction while entertaining using comedy, horror, drama, and the like, films offer a way to examine challenging, and at times, painful experiences. "Inviting film, a source of entertainment to many, to illustrate the presence of psychological dynamics creates an environment that provides a comfortable space for individuals to engage intimately with psychological concepts and foster inspiring connections that can be otherwise overlooked" (Marshall Woods, 2018, p. 16). "People can use entertainment not only as a way of experiencing enjoyment, but also as a means of grappling with questions such as life's purpose and meaningfulness" (de Leeuw & Buijzen, 2016, p. 43). Using film in this manner asks audience members to consider film not only as a source of enjoyment, but as an opportunity to learn.

Because film lends itself to exploration within its audience members, film and psychology is most prevalently seen within academic settings as a teaching tool. Within university and professional studies, it is not unlikely to enroll in an abnormal psychology or psychopathology course that relies heavily upon film analysis (Bluestone, 2000). "Movies have been used as a helpful adjunct with a variety of student populations such as undergraduate and graduate psychology students; medical students; and students in nursing, occupational therapy and pharmacy programs" (Niemiec, 2007, p. 2). Films tend to offer students a way of observing "behavior in greater complexity, more imbedded within the social world, then [*sic*] do other modes of presentation" (Bolt, 1976; Anderson, 1992, p. 155). In theory, the audience is placed in the filmmakers' creation of a "subjective, artistic worldview" and audiences are provided "with meaning for the behavior that the film portrays" (Anderson, 1992, p. 155; Miller, 1987), which allows this craft to be ideal for making topics within courses "immediate, relevant and concrete" for students (Anderson, 1992, p. 155; Fleming et al., 1990; Kinney, 1975; Nissim-Sabat, 1979). Furthermore, films provide pupils the opportunity to view psychiatric diagnostic criteria and the ways in which such conditions manifest, utilize psychopathology theory to understand the richness of what is viewed, and offer recommendations for treatment in the absence of the pressure to do no harm to an actual patient (Fleming et al., 1990). This method of teaching has been quite effective, and when done well, films have had a way of staying with students over time.

Bucciferro (2021) states that a film is a "cultural product", one that provides "not only narrative complexity but also symbolic connections to the larger social and political realms" (p. 171). As a psychologist, within this field, we follow the ethical requirements to enhance cultural awareness and sensitivity; and film has historically been a vehicle to provide narratives for conversations to discuss challenging topics within professional learning spaces often and freely. These have included, but are not limited to, educational institutions that are charged with teaching psychological dynamics where films are used to elucidate various psychological occurrences and disturbances. For instance, the Washington Baltimore Center for Psychoanalysis in partnership with The George Washington University's Professional Psychology Program hosts numerous continuing education courses annually amongst peers entitled Psychoanalytics Takes on Cinema. In this setting, licensed mental health professionals from around the world examine the psychological nuances and characters found within feature films. This venture to utilize film productions in an

Introduction 5

educational manner has gained such popularity that American Psychological Association, Division 39 (Society for Psychoanalysis and Psychoanalytic Psychology) has also birthed an educational program with the use of film entitled Cinematic Imprints, allowing filmmakers to speak directly with mental health professionals for a bidirectional conversation regarding the development of the creative piece while understanding the film through a psychoanalytical lens. Thus, during academic matriculation, many students and professionals are introduced to the influence of psychology in film vicariously to their learning objectives.

A Psychological Connection

We patronize "the cinema to experience mirth, compassion, sadness, bittersweet emotions, thrill, horror, and soon [*sic*] in response to what we see and hear happening to characters and ourselves" (Tan, 2018, p. 11). Characters who are relatable allow the audience to align with the conflicts held by the characters in a manner that states, "if this were to happen in life, this is one way in which I could manage the issue". Holding conflict at a distance and separate from the state of our lives creates a safe space to tolerate the intolerable. Screening films that viewers can relate to allows one to call upon the defense mechanism of displacement that protects one from being overcome by difficult feelings that surface in the face of emotional experiences. Displacement is a higher-level neurotic defense, one that is classified as sophisticated, mature, and a healthy way of managing life's challenges (Gabbard, 2005; Marshall Woods, 2018). This way of coping supports a person in their ability to move their "emotion, preoccupation, or behavior from its initial or natural object to another because its original direction is for some reason anxiety ridden" (McWilliams, 2011, p. 139). This occurs "when one experiences a feeling that poses a threat of discomfort, to resume a comfortable state, one may express the feeling through an alternative vehicle" (Marshall Woods, 2018, p. 16) such as using what is witnessed in film. Rather than feel uneasy regarding an experience, individuals are able to examine a similar occurrence in life within the narratives film provide. This defense mechanism helps audiences have motivation to engage in further contemplation into the conflict knowing that their situation is not outside the norm and has the ability to be worked through. This particular defense mechanism becomes an important auxiliary agent in processing what is viewed within film, where audiences are able to apply what is seen and integrate what is adopted into one's understanding of self with greater ease.

"Movies are simulations of real life and even though the viewer knows they represent a fictitious reality, they can induce changes in behavior, perception, and physiology" (Benedetti, 2021, p. 275). In fact, according to Kinreich et al. (2011) and Yoshihara et al. (2016) as cited in Benedetti (2021), "the changes that are produced range from autonomic activation to emotional distress and from cognition to behavior and the changes are associated with changes in brain activity" (p. 275). For instance, "narrative fiction, in particular, helps us to understand ourselves, to think—emotionally, imaginatively, reflectively—about human behavior, and to step outside

6 Introduction

the immediate pressures and the automatic reactions of the moment" (Boyd, 2009, p. 208). The power film has to introduce new concepts to audiences' minds, hearts, and souls is extraordinary and can be a catalyst for facilitating human evolution.

Open to All

Since I began working in the intersection of film and psychology, it has not been uncommon for me to hear, "I do what you do on my sofa while watching films. I analyze the characters and think about them after and wonder what if…". Yes, this behavior is encouraged! To take time to contemplate and internalize what has been seen is time well spent in my view. And, though folk psychology, as character-ized as, "film spectators, filmmakers, critics, and scholars, untutored and intuitive psychology" (Plantinga, 2011, p. 26), "is sometimes thought to be insufficiently theoretical, inaccurate, prone to the idiosyncratic responses of individuals" (Plant-inga, 2011, p. 27), engaging in personal contemplation once viewing a film "has a therapeutic value" (Plantinga, 2011, p. 27). "'Folk psychology' we unreflectively use every day in order to predict and explain the behavior of others and perhaps of ourselves" (Currie, 2004, p. 108). Through film watching, "audiences come to understand something about themselves" (Plantinga, 2011, p. 32). Plantinga (2011) continues, "the goal for film scholars ought not to be to wholly avoid folk psychol-ogy; but rather to correct and supplement it with the tools of scientific psychol-ogy and philosophical analysis" (p. 46). Theorists suggest that "it is a mistake to think that we can speak and write productively about the experience of film only by appealing to a 'deep' psychological theory, that is one which postulates states, processes, and mechanisms not acknowledged by our quotidian psychological knowledge" (Currie, 2004, p. 108). This has certainly been the approach that I most desire to utilize when consulting on films with filmmakers. A "folk psychological" approach is used to draft the characters and themes in scripts by the filmmaker; and specific psychological theory is used to enhance their art.

In my journey as a psychologist with a special interest in film, I too was a participant conceptualizing films through a folk psychological lens in the past. I invite you to engage from the position you find yourself in currently. Similarly to the recommendation offered in the book *Best Psychology in Film* (Marshall Woods, 2018), it is encouraged that you watch the films that are discussed to provide con-text to the content in each chapter exploring decades of African American film works through a psychodynamic lens. Fully engaging with the art of film that in-cludes dance and song is equally encouraged; thus, a playlist for this book can be found on Spotify ("Black Film from a Psychodynamic Lens"). Screening each film, I hope, will make for a cocreated entertaining and meaningful read.

Disclaimer

The films offered in this book and acknowledged in each decade are only a few of the African American films that were worthy of psychological exploration. Most of these films discussed are well known in and outside of the African American community, remain in common conversations in social circles, and are included in recaps of the most influential films of the allotted decade. Unfortunately, in order to include all films within the last 50 years would have made for quite a longer book published. Yet, this comes with the fortunate reality that not all great African American films are included in this book. This limitation of the book reflects the progress made in the industry, where the sheer number of films created and produced to distribution is so great that one book could not capture all of the art contributing to African American culture. Their lack of presence in this piece of literature does not, in any way, shrink the influence and importance of the art. Those films included, however, are films that have globally touched the hearts of most and have left indelible imprints upon viewers' psyches, making them the classic films that they are.

1

Ease on Down the Road?

In true psychodynamic soil, we root ourselves in the quest to understand the present, holding the importance of examining the influence of the past to inform the future that we desire to have. As media—television, advertisements, social media, video games, alternative and virtual realities, and film, to include documentaries and feature films—have been birthed and grown in their existence, they currently saturate our lives. Today, we have the opportunity to engage in media on demand and they are available at every turn. Media are present on our personal mobile devices and on the sides of bus terminals while we are waiting for public transportation. Though all of the media platforms noted have the power to be influential in our lives, special attention is paid to film. Feature films "often have complex characters with symptoms depicted in the context of an intricate plot" (Bluestone, 2000, p. 142). The medium of motion pictures has set the stage for the narrative storytelling we find in other media sources today.

And what a magical invention film has been. "Film viewers take part in a playful simulation in which the film leads them to imagine they are present in a fictional world, where they witness fictional events that film characters are involved in" (Tan, 2018, p. 11). Films offer the opportunity to portray individuals in their exact likeness to all with access of viewing the footage. Psychologically, what a promising innovation. Whether fiction or nonfiction, one can use film to share with others a specific narrative that provides twinship suggesting that there are others who have similar experiences to the creator of the media source. The narratives depicted in films facilitate understanding differences amongst people in a manner that can promote curiosity and compassion while demystifying others' beliefs, culture, and existence. Viewers of film are invited to become engrossed with the visual and musical thematic narratives, and through this intense attention yields empathy and identification with the characters (Tan, 2018; Zillmann, 1991; Cohen, 2001). As a result, it is important that film is all-inclusive. Stories of individuals of all ages, races, ethnicities, genders, socioeconomic status, and abilities have a place in cinema. They can share unique human experiences with others, which underscores that "movies can have a significant impact on gender and ethnic stereotypes, change attitudes towards certain groups of people and cause newly formed opinions on various issues" (Kubrak, 2020, p. 2). Indeed, film has an allure that

DOI: 10.4324/9781003399902-2

gently captivates one's attention, while opening eyes and minds wider to what the world holds within.

The birth of Hollywood in the 1920s began creating films where "all manipulations of the camera, lighting, editing and sets should be transparent, unnoticed by the filmgoer" (Cutting, 2007, p. 9). However, the construction of the road into these Hollywood films has not always been a golden path for all who have traveled. Rather, "for blacks in American movies, it's been a long, sometimes turbulent, and often rocky journey throughout the twentieth century, into the twenty-first" (Bogle, 2019, p. xiii). Prior to the twentieth century, within silent film works, African Americans graced films on and off the screen in a manner that added to the richness of productions in a multitude of ways. Black film has had an extensive history with significant accomplishments in the film industry. "Through their achievements in the dramatic arts, African Americans have broken barriers, enriched American culture, and inspired audiences around the world" (National Museum of African American History and Culture, 2023). However, in Hollywood in the 1920s, "film roles requiring the portrayal of black characters were almost non-existent" (Verney, 2003, p. 19). Verney continues, "the few parts that were available were almost always as servants, maids, or chauffeurs and involved only brief appearances. A slight advance was that by the end of the decade these were usually played by African Americans rather than whites in blackface" (p. 19).

With the liberty that has been experienced within the African American community to create and share film productions with others, it has inspired filmmakers to utilize their craft in the service of evolution both socially and politically. African American filmmakers have created stories to share the diversity of experiences African American individuals have had navigating life in America. It is with these stories and films that filmmakers have generously provided their perspectives about the world in which they live to provide others the opportunity to share a piece of what they have experienced. Some of these stories have emotionally and psychologically difficult storylines, ones that are disheartening, even traumatic. And yet, filmmakers vulnerably create a window for audiences to view a part of themselves within the art and to walk away enlightened, and forever changed. This process, of consciously recognizing the challenge one has faced, emotionally experiencing the affect that arises from said conflict, and sharing the experience with others in a transformed, healthy manner, such as art, allows audiences to witness filmmakers' defense mechanisms at work; in particular sublimation. Specifically, the American Psychological Association (APA) defines this term as, "in classical psychoanalytic theory, a defense mechanism in which unacceptable sexual or aggressive drives are unconsciously channeled into socially acceptable modes of expression and redirected into new, learned behaviors, which indirectly provide some satisfaction for the original drives" (2018a). Psychodynamically, we understand sublimation to also be a defense mechanism utilized unconsciously, yet it acts in a manner that reduces anxieties that are a consequence of unacceptable urges or harmful stimuli (Hockenbury & Hockenbury, 2008). Due to the use of this healthy and what is referred to by Gabbard (2005) as a mature defense, we delight in the creations of filmmakers and learn vicariously from their personal experience and imagination.

10   Ease on Down the Road?

Further, sublimation is frequently utilized to resolve emotionally conflictual situations while evoking larger than personal change. For instance, filmmakers have created films that depict life as an African American individual in America that leave audiences with many questions to wrestle and contend with. A few inquiries contemplated after film screenings include: "What are my perceptions of Black people?", "How are Black people treated in America?", and "How might one be complacent in such treatment of this minority group?". Over the decades we have viewed how "the roles that black artists played on the stage and screen reflected changing aspirations, struggles and realities for black people in American society" (National Museum of African American History and Culture, 2023). These images within cinema best reflect the persistent yet shifting fragile landscape in America for African American people and allow for increased exposure of individuals' life experiences while inspiring the facilitation of greater awareness and social change. Further, with exploration of films in the past, we have an account of what may have been important for filmmakers to share with audiences of that time. These films have left behind a historical record capturing the happenings and their perception of events of a certain era, providing audiences an opportunity to revisit events years, decades, and now, a century later.

Lastly, filmmaking also invites wonderances into fantasy. "Münsterberg observed that the film audience's enjoyment is due to prolonged states of attention strongly focused on a fictional story-world, so strong, in fact that the here and now escapes consciousness and it seems instead as if an 'outer world were woven into our mind'" (Tan, 2018, p. 10). By doing so, audiences are able to provide a pause on everyday life and lean into being entertained. This process lends itself to escapism, specifically "the tendency to escape from the real world to the delight or security of a fantasy world" (APA, 2018b). Though escapism may reflect a less sophisticated defensive way of managing feelings that surface through a film screening, its utility may be welcomed in providing a space away from the realities of racism, discrimination, and the injustices of the world.

Motion Pictures' Influence

Films have always been a big hit with the public. The presence of individuals of color in film has been a consistent desire. Whether hiring African Americans or standing in white individuals in "black face" to be perceived as African American, having the presence of Black people has been critical to storytelling through film's history—though complicated, as many times the intent of these films included "the appropriation of African American culture by white entertainers in a way that maximized negative stereotypes" (Verney, 2003, p. 3). Presently, cinema is a widely supported source of entertainment globally. Within America alone, films gross over three trillion dollars annually (Box Office Mojo, 2022), and individual films can earn hundreds of millions of dollars during the opening weekend. Since the Covid-19 pandemic, films have gained momentum in engagement as individuals bore in place for safety for themselves and others. Watching films in the comfort of one's home ordered upon streaming platforms supported film and filmmakers while entertaining the public during a time of fear and grief. With these many eyes on film works, it continues to make this artform "a powerful vehicle" that exposes individuals to: different ways of life, alternative approaches to manage situations and varying means to relate to others. Further, what is found within cinema is a rich depiction of influential narratives and tales found within the scripts and performances of characters and can offer a fertile ground to understand the manner in which people see the world and persons within it (Marshall Woods, 2018, p. 14). Due to the seismic influence of film, the content, what is presented, and how it is portrayed are all questions in discussion and continue to warrant attention. When these conversations are not had, media can provide, and have historically provided, the public with discouraging, damaging images to one's self-concept and self-esteem.

Because of the great influence film has upon audiences, representation in film that is inclusive is as important as its content. Within the 1890s, "The silent era", for African Americans, "movies were a parade of embarrassing, insulting, demeaning caricatures—often offsprings of the rigid stereotypes of the minstrel shows" (Bogle, 2019, p. 3) that gained audiences' attention. These films boasted what are understood as familiar racial tropes of African Americans that perpetuated roles such "as a comic, childlike, often enough grotesque Dark Other—an oddity in American life and culture" (Bogle, 2019, p. 3). Whether adult or a child actor, individuals were cast in stereotypical, often unbilled roles for their contributions. For those interested in making films a career, one learned that there were costs to being included in the industry. Naturally, many questioned whether the reward was worth what price was required to take part.

The Price of Hollywood

Individuals of color have held concerns regarding the manner in which we have been portrayed in the media for a century. Whether through 1920s cartoons depicting individuals of various shapes and sizes possessing large facial features enjoying watermelon in fellowship, or through present-day films with individuals displaying racially informed tropes of how Black and brown persons have been cast and scripted, there has been an understanding that these images have had lasting impressions. Though the practice of placing people of color into racist caricatures in film has been a quotidian experience, we have had thought leaders over the most recent decades who have used their platform to articulate the ways in which people of color have been represented within film. bell hooks, West (2008), Alexander (2019), and the like have pioneered speaking to these stereotypical tropes found within film and media works. In recognizing and naming these stereotypical roles, we are able to become conscientious audiences to the material we are presented to absorb. For example, Alexander (2019) astutely noted that, "black women were particularly susceptible to cinematic stereotyping based upon American antebellum notions of black womanhood" (p. 839). These limiting roles offered performers opportunities to enact a similar role repeatedly that lacked complexity and nuance.

Because of the prevalence of these roles, various labels have been assigned to create better recognition of what is present within cinematic works.

For example, Carolyn West's work notes that redundant stereotypes depicted in film have included the Mammy, Jezebel, and/or Sapphire (West, 2008). Kelly and Greene (2010) specified that the "sapphire" stereotype was created later by 1950s television and exhibited the Black woman as a chronically unhappy, "angry, hostile, aggressive wife" (p. 189) in the absence of considering the source of her negatively held affect. As the Jezebel is characterized as a hypersexual woman, the Mammy is loyal to serving her white masters and more recently her white employers. Let's explore these tropes with greater detail while considering the impact these figures can have upon viewers.

The Sapphire being an upset woman supported the belief that women of African American descent presented with what was familiarly referred to as "attitudinal". These women can present as unpartnered and appear angrily aggravated with the world. Due to their negative affect, they are portrayed as interpersonal poison. They present as fatigued by their frustrations and men are fatigued by their complaints. What is not readily depicted is the complexity of this character that includes her own fatigue in managing her responsibilities in the lack of assistance, managing responsibilities due to feelings of obligation, and struggles with her desire to be able to generate new social and intimate relationships that have the potential to be fulfilling and healing due to her lack of energy to give anything further to herself at the end of the day. Her "attitude" that is serviced in sass masks sorrow, regret, fear, sadness, loneliness, hurt, and pain that she may not readily allow others to see in her. She is aware that being vulnerable may cause her defensive walls to implode with no guarantee her defenses will reconstruct when she requires them. This role can be viewed within characters such as Angela's character in Tyler Perry's film *Why Did I Get Married?* (2007) and Joanna's character in Tyler Perry's film *For Colored Girls* (2010).

The mammy stereotype is the "most pervasive image of Black women" (Warren-Gordon & McMillan, 2022, p. 249). It is a concept with an etiology that captures a Black woman's ability to care for White people selfishly, raising their children and supporting the adults during distressing times. She is typically portrayed as a physically larger-build woman, emotionally expressive while asexual in manner, jolly, lacking threat to the White woman of the household, "having dark skin, a wide nose, dressing in bandanna clothing, and always wearing an apron" (Warren-Gordon & McMillan, 2022, p. 249). "The character of the household cook became one of the earliest representations of the jovial, rotund, black mammy, a figure hitherto uncommon" (Verney, 2003, p. 18). Though the Mammy cares for her employer's children, it is at the neglect of being available to her own family. She is seemingly grateful for the sacrifices she makes to care for her family financially despite their challenges, which, at times, places her self-respect and dignity in compromised positions. Her commitment to her employment is unwavering; she doesn't just care for the white children in the household, she loves them through their unfair, unloving, racist behaviors that she endures from them. She offers a listening ear to and even pities the white adults who are portrayed as requiring assistance to navigate everyday life situations, that are, in comparison to her financial challenges, sociopolitical conflicts and chronic exposures to trauma appear inconsequential. Being a stereotype born from slavery times, the Mammy continues to place the Black woman in a position of servitude. By the 1930s the mammy stereotype was challenged and by the 1940s there were both an articulated desire and a demand for greater complexity in roles for African American women and Hollywood seemed to understand there was an audience for such evolved films (Bogle, 2019). Despite shifts, the mammy expression can be viewed across generations of film and Alexander (2019) argues that remnants of this trope continued to be perpetuated in modern film as late as the beloved 2008 film work of *Sex and the City* in the character Louise performed by Jennifer Hudson.

Further, the Jezebel representation of Black women originated similarly through slavery and was primarily used in a manner so as to rationalize white males' victimization of enslaved females (Pilgrim, 2012). Specifically, the Jezebel was portrayed as hypersexual, possessing sexual desires that were insatiable (Jerald et al., 2017; Pilgrim, 2012). As a result, Jezebels were not sexually fulfilled by African American men and thus were justified to engage in sexual pleasures with White men. Black women were viewed as dangerous seductresses who could take a man's power from him and be in control, which supports all the reasons why these women needed to be controlled (Warren-Gordon & McMillan, 2022). Images of the Jezebel were visually present in trinkets, media, and music. Though this stereotype has been extinguished from being placed on concrete items, the Jezebel continues to perpetuate in mainstream media where Black women are "more likely to appear in provocative clothing and to appear oversexualized in music videos compared to white women" (Turner, 2011; Warren-Gordon & McMillan, 2022, p. 249).

Each of these tropes holds negative projections of Black women. Equally, these tropes are utilized to portray Black women in a contained, unidimensional, unrealistic manner. The impressions they leave upon audiences have contributed to the construction of individuals' self-esteem and have helped shape beliefs regarding one's self-concept as a person of color in America. It has influenced how we understand our relation to our white neighbors and how we understand ourselves within our fellow Black communities of individuals of all shades of black and brown. These impressions have not only influenced POC, but have influenced how individuals of color are treated by counterparts and within systems. For example, researchers such as Hampton et al. (2003), Olive (2012), Gooden (1980), Gillum (2002), and Niemann et al. (1994) have found that media images contribute to Black women's experiences of lower conviction rates when victimized in Black-on-Black rape when compared to other race and ethnicity rape cases, inculcating the belief that Black women are sexually promiscuous and aggressive which in turn reduces the inhibition against acting out physically on women and allows men to rationalize being violent against them. As such, creating constructs that suggest specific individuals have limited ways in which they can behave, think, feel, and belong in the world facilitates fixed perceptions to occur, leading to fixed reactions and interpersonal relations that follow.

And, our Black men? Men globally have had greater privileges within film. For example, films with male leads have larger budgets, which in turn leads to greater earned revenue. Additionally, as men age, they remain viable for being cast in a diverse set of roles and are provided greater opportunity to have speaking roles that leave a greater influence upon the audience (Yang et al., 2020). Yet, Black men continue to have difficulty breaking free from the "traditional masculinity, often violently expressed" roles offered (Eschholz et al., 2002, p. 325). Similarly, Black men have been placed into commonplace tropes, though not as much attention has been paid to these categories which they have occupied. Bucciferro (2021) offers that "African American men are often cast for roles that connect them to crime, homelessness, drugs, and various social problems or as minstrelsy characters offering comic relief" (p. 172). "Thus, we see a picture of a macho black male emerging from movies" (Eschholz et al., 2002, p. 321).

Unfortunately, the stereotypical tropes that have been recognized for African American individuals are similarly found within film for other ethnicities as well. It is important to note that it has not only been African American individuals impacted in disparaging ways in the history of cinematic works. Specifically, "Hispanics, Asians, Native Americans, and other minorities are rarely shown in leading roles in popular film" (Eschholz et al., 2002, p. 322). The results echo the negative impact that these tropes have on individuals and communities alike. For instance, the Latinx community has experienced similar difficulties with representation within the film industry, where Román (2000) noted "Hollywood does not exclude" the Latinx community in films (p. 43). Rather, "the themes are the same, and the roles are typically narrow, shallow caricatures that purportedly represent their entire community" (Román, 2000, p. 42), portraying individuals as "hot-blooded" gang members, lovers, or musicians (Román, 2000, p. 42), criminals, or undocumented immigrants (Bernhardt, 2021; Román, 2000). Additionally, Paner (2018) reported, for example, "historically, if Asians are not portrayed in a stereotypical role, then they are given no role at all, rendered invisible by Hollywood and mass audiences" (p. 3). When included in productions, "Hollywood also has a habit of indiscriminately casting any Asian in any Asian role; a Chinese actor may portray a Korean character, and vice versa. This perpetuates the idea that Asia is a monolith with interchangeable cultures" (Paner, 2018, p. 6). Additionally, women in particular are assigned damaging tropes to enact in cinemas that include "a cold and dangerous villain", "a mindless, simpering doll", and as one "eager to please their white lord and master" (Rajgopal, 2010, p. 149; Marshall Woods, 2024). And, similarly, Native Americans struggle to be represented and are typically depicted using negative stereotypes that include portrayals of the "savage", "uneducated", "poor", "drunken", "angry", "aggressive", "stupid", "inferior", and "lazy" (Mihelich, 2001, p. 130). "Positive" stereotypes are also employed in films that highlight Native American culture that include "proud", "noble", "spiritual", "deeply religious", "wise", "nature-loving", and "traditional" persons (Mihelich, 2001, p. 130). Films also portray Native Americans limited to the setting of a "Native casino" (McLaurin, 2012, p. 50), "which places visual and narrative boundaries to the spaces that Native Americans are shown navigating America" (Marshall Woods, 2024, p. 139). If "film is a common entertainment form that fulfills the audience's desire to make emotional connections with characters and learn about their social world" (Yang et al., 2020, p. 30:1), then we must surmise that our efforts regarding the formation of scripts, the roles requested, and the art created are called to reduce and ultimately extinguish these stereotypical ways of imagining others.

Gathering the Golden Bricks

Within the early cinema years, filmmakers did not imagine that African Americans were able to represent themselves within films (Bogle, 2019). Consequently, African Americans were portrayed by actors adorned in Max Factor Pan-Cake makeup, "better referred to as 'blackface'", used to "alter the appearance of actors, who were most often white, when they performed as stereotypical Black characters" (Academy Museum). These actors enacted a projected account of people of color, what was believed regarding how African Americans behaved and functioned in the world. The roles they occupied tended to include a minstrel role or portray individuals exhibiting atrocities. For example, as no book that addresses a history of film can neglect, *The Birth of a Nation* (1915) provided audiences with a narrative that supported and uplifted traumatic experiences by the Ku Klux Klan, bringing an African American man (a white male actor in blackface) to "justice" by a lynching. Within other film productions, white individuals with blackface moved, danced, and spoke in dialects that reflected projections of how African Americans were perceived by white communities. These projections, which served as a form of entertainment, manifested in acting out behaviors and were acts of both humiliation and appropriation.

There is a "body of evidence [that] suggests it has been typical for media to either utilize stereotypes disparaging females and minorities and thereby perpetrate myths concerning their existence or to completely exclude them, implying that members of these groups occupy no significant social space" (Eschholz et al., 2002, p. 300). Within the history of film, both offenses occurred equally. Displaying stereotypical behaviors securing myths regarding African Americans' behaviors while excluding African Americans from productions by employing white actors to portray people of color suggests that film served to enable individuals to reflect the events of the world while actualizing fantasies of the filmmaker to be shared with the public both cathartically and for propaganda.

Creating Space, Race Films

"During the silent era, African American entrepreneurs launched a number of independent film companies" (National Museum of African American History and Culture, 2023). These production companies were invested in sharing narratives with audiences "that saluted African American heroism and achievement, or that presented nuanced expressions of struggle and triumph" (Bogle, 2019, p. 5). Because of the segregation African Americans experienced within the film industry from 1910 through the 1940s, "actors rarely appeared on the Hollywood screen except in musical or servant roles. But 'race movies' depicted a wide range of Black characters and experiences, from middle class families to gangsters and cowboys" (National Museum of African American History and Culture, 2023). These films included varying genres of westerns, adventure, comedies, and drama and employed African Americans as actors and screenwriters. Race films created outside of Hollywood can be accredited with offering numerous filmmakers and artists the ability to gain employment in the industry (Bogle, 2019). "Despite the social and cultural barriers of racial violence and discrimination, this was a fertile period for Black storytelling, producing movies inspired and appreciated by Black communities, many of which dealt with the manifold impacts of segregation" (Academy Museum, 2023). The success of these films was so great that a number of actors involved successfully moved into the Hollywood arena. Together George and "Noble Johnson's Lincoln Motion Pictures Company and [Oscar] Micheaux gave birth to independent black cinema and what came to be known as 'race movies'" (Bogle, 2019, p. 9), touching audiences intended to share in racial identity and including awareness of and accurate acknowledgments to the culture. Between the years of 1915 and 1948, an estimated 150 independent companies both produced and distributed "race film" that "offered an array of stories and roles for Black actors and were aimed at Black audiences" (Academy Museum, 2023).

George and Noble Johnson's Lincoln Motion Pictures Company

The Lincoln Motion Pictures Company was a frontrunner in the development of race films. Being one of the first Black-owned production companies, it was an influential artistic house (est. 1915 in Los Angeles) for these films. Noble M. Johnson along with his brother George P. Johnson, who joined the company a year into its establishment, crafted a number of early films that "promoted ideas of racial uplift and were notable for their nuanced portrayals of Black middle class" (Academy Museum, 2023). Financial challenges forced The Lincoln Motion Pictures Company to conclude its contribution to the film industry in 1923, though within its duration it set the stage for future filmmakers to emulate its works.

Oscar Micheaux (1884–1951)

Within his era, race films contributed significantly to the film industry. "Between 1919 and 1948 Micheaux wrote, directed, and produced approximately 40 films" (National Museum of African American History and Culture, 2023). Though not originally a filmmaker, rather a self-published novelist, he produced his first film as a result of the lack of support he received to direct his own film from the company that desired to obtain his story (The Lincoln Motion Pictures Company). Based upon his influence on African American cinema, he was recognized as "the most successful independent filmmaker" (National Museum of African American

History and Culture, 2023) of his time due to his business savvy that exceeded his filmmaking abilities. Oscar Micheaux was aware of how to manage marketing and sales that facilitated his films to be seen. He worked to promote his films, collaborating with theater owners directly to manage the financing, distribution, and marketing of his films. His work included movies that mirrored popular films made in Hollywood; however, his films also included subjects depicting racial injustices in America such as lynchings, religion, interracial sex, and intraracial prejudices that exist within the African American community (National Museum of African American History and Culture, 2023). A number of his films bravely described the above events and social dynamics that were considered taboo for the time. As a result, his work is often described as "empowering and controversial", "daring, complicated and influential" (Academy Museum, 2023).

"Often we may find it hard to fathom how past moviegoers could have accepted Hollywood's stereotyped view of black America" (Bogle, 2019, p. xiii). Similarly, when reviewing the history, it can be difficult to understand why African Americans in the industry accepted such roles, including those that often were unbilled. As actress Hattie McDaniel stated, "I'd rather play a maid and make $700 a week than be one for $7" (National Museum of African American History and Culture, 2023). There was a conscious awareness among African Americans in the industry and by the 1940s some studio heads understood how the impact of viewing individuals consistently within a particular light limited how individuals could conceive of African Americans in the absence of interfacing with varying individuals on a personal level. Further, "media consumers inundated with unrealistic portrayals of females and minorities may be more likely to adopt cultural double standards based on race and sex" (Eschholz et al., 2002, p. 300).

Feet entered new doors that led actors onto different paths. For example, Hattie McDaniel's ability to engage in the roles she was afforded enabled her to be the first African American to win the highest esteemed Academy of Motion Pictures Award, an Oscar. Some filmmakers and performers used their position of power to advocate, being adamant that their voices be both heard and respected. For instance, Clarence Muse, an actor in the 1940s, was thoughtful regarding managing his image and working to reduce discrimination on set. However, the bricks of this path were heavy; they cut and injured many. The contributions that created the foundation for the road for individuals in the film industry today were known to be a rocky path—one requiring the use of psychological protective factors. As such, Lena Horne noted, "The image I chose to give is of a woman the audience can't reach and therefore can't hurt. They were not getting *me*, just a singer" (source unknown, located in Bogle, 2019, p. 74).

Paving the Way

By the 1950s "a new image of African Americans in the movies" arrived; "an intelligent, disciplined, dignified young black man, who lives by a code of fundamental decency and integrity" (Bogle, 2019, p. 93), was portrayed by Sydney Poitier.

Characters he enacted represented the anticipation of an integrated America (Bogle, 2019). However, shifts were brewing in America leading to unrest with civil rights wanting and women's rights longed for:

> In light of societal changes made possible by the civil rights and women's rights movement of the 1960s and 1970s, such as increased minority political participation, greater female control over reproduction, and passage of legislation to protect both groups from criminal victimization it seems logical that diversity in films would follow.
>
> (Eschholz et al., 2002, p. 303)

In fact, the year Martin Luther King, Jr. delivered his "I have a Dream Speech", 1963, Sydney Poitier earned an Academy Award for Best Actor. By the mid-1960s characters that placed African Americans in a submissive role were no longer as well received. Rather than idealized figures, audiences at this time and well into the 1970s desired "bold, assertive heroes who challenged the status quo and were ready for a day of racial reckoning" (Bogle, 2019, p. 139).

And that is what audiences received. In the 1970s African American film included ways to highlight African American culture through the use of drama and comedy in what is referred to as Blaxploitation cinema. As the United States experienced the riots of the 1960s, films of the 1970s highlighted social injustices and political views through strong characters with greater nuance. As a result, audiences could readily identify with the roles and were conscientious and thoughtful to examine the need to dismantle systems that fed into discrimination. These films were known to have "cultural markers, signifiers, references, and tropes speaking directly to the African American audience" (Bogle, 2019, p. 141). Additionally, and not unfamiliar with the past, these films often placed front and center the libidinal fantasies of the African American male towards females, representing females in similar less developed characters as in yesteryear. Despite this, in later years within the 1970s, African American females' roles began to catch up, and finally, the demand of complex roles was granted. Consequently, audiences were able to identify with these female characters who were portrayed defying standards previously held for women and welcomed these characters' ability to care for themselves, excel independently, and have the skills, wit, and determination to protect themselves in the world. Women such as Pam Grier, Cicely Tyson, Diana Ross, and Diahann Carroll led the charge in roles that provided characters that ranged from representing the life of a famous singer (*Lady Sings The Blues*, 1972) to fantastical heroines that had the ability to manage any trouble that came her way (*Foxy Brown*, 1974).

Black Film Through a Psychodynamic Lens

The following chapters approach African American cinema from the last five decades from a psychodynamic lens. In examining main themes, and characters' presentations, within films using psychodynamic theory we are able to elucidate various explicit takeaways from the films while uncovering implicit aspects that equally contribute to the films' charm.

Our Legacy

> "History is not the past. It is the present. We carry our history with us. We are our history."
> (James Baldwin, 1980)

Filmmakers' desire to dedicate work to honoring past trailblazers has been a staple within the repertoire of Black film. While observing the progression of African American people within the United States, it is important for energy to be directed to remembering our ancestors. We are the result of their struggles and successes, all Americans. Within film we are offered the ability to view and acknowledge intrapsychically what has been important in the minds of people of color in America to share with others. In each decade we naturally see filmmakers' interest to dedicate work to honor the legacies created by extraordinary people within extraordinary circumstances while honoring their humanity. Equally, as we are able to examine films in retrospect in this book, we can see that the films that were greenlit for a specific time shared and depicted an illustration of how our heroic ancestors experienced, navigated, and excelled within situations that reflected the global themes of a specific decade. Moreover, films highlighted within sections entitled "Legacy Films" will showcase the individuals that filmmakers needed to tell and remind the world about. It is also in this spirit that we honor the sentiments of psychodynamic theorists who acknowledge that the past is the foundation of our understanding of our current selves and informs our future being.

Lastly, similarly to my previous book, *Best Psychology in Film*, I stand by encouraging readers of this book to engage fully in a courtship with the material that will end with the union of these two disciplines, psychology and Black cinema. Investing time in screening each film mentioned within the book and thinking about the cinematic work together can significantly enrich the experience. Plantinga (2011) astutely offers that we understand characters "as persons" (p. 32) providing an opportunity for us to relate to the characters, rest in the themes, and ponder upon how the collective artistries influence film to make meaningful imprints on our lives.

2

Living Black (1980–1989)

Cinema in the 1980s told tales that illustrated the lives of individuals of color in the United States. Within the early years of the 80s, films depicted how individuals of color navigated America in the absence of "deep seated racial tension" (Bogle, 2019, p. 165). These films uniquely captivated audiences by showing the love of African American culture that included innovative artistic talents furthering the development of hip hop, Black Greek life, and narratives of perseverance, courage, and triumph. Filmmakers such as Robert Townsend and Spike Lee became significant independent contributors beginning in this era with *She's Gotta Have It* (1986), *Hollywood Shuffle* (1987), and *Do the Right Thing* (1989); all films that continue to provide a thought-provoking richness to understanding views of feminism, interpersonal relations between and within race, and how individuals perceive ethnicity and gender in America. Lee stated, "I wanted to attempt to capture the richness of African American culture that I can see, just standing on the corner, or looking out of my window every day and try to get that on screen" (National Museum of African American History and Culture, 2023).

Within this era, love stories highlighted the complicated dynamics in African American communities. The narratives' underlying themes revealed that love could be riddled with complex dynamics that can challenge and make for prolonged unhealthy relationships. These films invited audiences to have open conversations about various types of relationships that may have been taboo historically. With a myriad of relationships depicted, individuals may have, for the first time, viewed upon the screen relationship dynamics mirroring their personal lived experience in a meaningful way.

The 1980s provide viewers a great number of films that place love at the forefront of the many themes generated within this age and suggest that there are limitless possibilities when one is able to love themselves and bestow the same love onto others. We see power and control within characters' relationships across this decade's work, highlighting when breaking free from power and control from a partner, and harnessing power and control over one's life, can not only provide a film that inspires empowerment, but lends itself to the reality of freedoms one can entertain for one's personal self.

Within these ten years, Black films were successfully able to capture the culture and capture countless experiences of what it could mean to be Black in America at

DOI: 10.4324/9781003399902-3

Living Black (1980–1989) 21

that time. Films accentuating elaborate expressions of new art forms of dance (pop locking, breakin', etc.), music (hip hop, rap), fashion, and visual art (graffiti) by the individuals that represented the development of the culture allowed individuals within these communities to be seen in a greater wholistic way. As the African American community was illustrated through satires, comedy, and laughter that many times had a return to Blaxploitation films (e.g. *I'm Gonna Git You Sucka*, 1988), these films also did not abort opportunities to reveal the significant difficulties, even trauma, in these same spaces. Poverty, lack of opportunities, police profiling, and social injustices were depicted that sometimes lacked scripting and relied upon film to show the viewer what life could be like for those with and for those without (i.e. *Krush Groove*, 1985; *Beat Street*, 1984). Using film in a manner to depict societal problems to audiences offers a near experience through displacement to depict and empathize with various ways in which people live life. And for all of its wealth, the 1980s also delivered productions to the public that continued to perpetuate racial stereotypes and put light to these dynamics present within film in ways that could not be ignored (*Hollywood Shuffle*, 1987; *Colors*, 1988).

Despite the positioning of the release dates of these films ranging from 1980 to 1989, these cinematic works resonated with moviegoers who enjoyed varying genres such as drama and a great deal of comedy. Engaging the audience in a manner to evoke laughter allowed theaters to become a cathartic, therapeutic space for the African American community. Specifically, the use of humor within cinema provides a healthy, higher-order defense to be used to offer lightness to themes that may have a consistent, striking, disheartened tone. Creating a film primarily with a comedic narrative allows the moviegoer to gain approximately two hours of emotional relief, that may be desired from the pressures of the world outside the theater. The realities of the struggles persons may have experienced within this decade were replicated through film. These films were readily received and depictions of African Americans invited a feeling of connection, community, and a continuation of race and Blaxploitation films exhibiting love for living Black in America. Welcome back to the 1980s.

A Soldier's Story (1984)

An adaption from Charles Fuller's Pulitzer Prize-winning play entitled "A Soldier's Play", Howard E. Rollins, Jr. (as Captain Davenport) and Adolph Caesar (depicting Sergeant Waters) star in this award-winning film that depicts the African American soldiers within the 221st Chemical Smoke Generator Battalion. The film begins with the death of Sergeant Waters where Captain Davenport is required to investigate his murder. Sergeant Waters was a respected leader, yet equally feared and disliked by his soldiers. In the presence of a stranger to the battalion, initial accounts by the soldiers of Sergeant Waters' leadership are provided that he was fair, though challenging. It is however realized within the three days Captain Davenport is given to investigate the murder that Sergeant Waters had a venomous disgust for African Americans and their portrayal of themselves. Due to the hate Sergeant

Waters deemed was unacceptable behavior by African Americans in an evolving nation, Sergeant Waters confided in Private Wilkie (acted by Art Evans) of his calculated manipulations towards soldiers when he felt their Black southern presentation was a threat to forward progression in America. In his account, he describes one experience had during World War I with a solider and a second experience with a member of his battalion that resulted in this soldier's incarceration and severe mental health demise resulting in suicide. The men of Sergeant Waters' battalion's rage ensued, albeit silently.

"The individual inculcation of the racist stereotypes, values, images, and ideologies perpetuated by the White dominant society about one's racial group, leading to feelings of self-doubt, disgust, and disrespect for one's race and/or oneself" is the manner in which Pyke (2010, p. 553) defines internalized racism. David et al. (2019) write, "early conceptualizations of internalized racism suggest that experiencing racism over lifetimes and generations can lead individuals to internalize the messages of inferiority they receive about their group, and to develop animosity toward others of the same race or ethnicity, or toward other oppressed racial or ethnic groups" (p. 1060). Sergeant Waters' abhorrence of individuals of color whom he perceived as using cultural representation to entertain people and successfully gain a gleeful audience was repulsive. As he described, his father also carried a similar disdain, allowing the impact of internalized racism to be understood as a multi-generational phenomenon for Sergeant Waters. The manner he experienced his revolt, the fixation he had once positioning his detestation into a targeted person, and the guileful plans he created coupled with rationalizations to justify his heinous acts against Black men, depicted the insidious and ungovernable nature that internalized racism can take.

The influence internalized racism has on an individual's psyche, self-esteem, and self-concept suggests that the internal malignancy one experiences is intolerable and grave. In an effort to disavow said shameful feelings one readily projects the venom onto others and experiences chronic contempt for those who share community. As David et al. (2019) noted, though research on internalized racism has increased, this specific dynamic remains an area that is worthy of special attention when conceptualizing racism as a global construct. Film has readily taken this topic for further contemplation, exhibition, and audiences' conversations. For example, only four years following, a second popular box office film explored and directly addressed internalized racism, as portrayed upon a college campus (*School Daze*, 1988) (to be found in Legacy Films).

Purple Rain (1984)

Home is one of the most prominent symbols of one's self and allows for one's interior psyche to be represented in one's exterior environment (Després, 1991). Early childhood attachments and exposure to human interactions within the home lay the foundation of how one experiences and navigates adult life. The home is typically where individuals learn what is considered "normal" within relationships with self and others. *Purple Rain* offers a narrative regarding the influence the home environment had upon a talented songwriter and performer, The Kid (performed by Prince), and his relationship with his employers, bandmates, and romantic interest Apollonia (acted by Apollonia Kotero). More specifically, *Purple Rain* depicts how an individual exposed to chronic domestic violence may respond to others within adult relationships.

For The Kid, home was a consistently unpredictable place. He resided in a home where his father spontaneously experienced anger and performed violent acts. Consequently, many times The Kid apprehensively approached his home, quietly listening at the door to determine the safety of the space. Would his father be in a fit of rage, and be found physically assaulting his mother? At times he arrived hearing the cries of his mother in abusive assaults by his father, where he responded by emotionally shifting into being the protector of his mother, entering the home, yet rapidly becoming the victim of his father's physical assaults. Other times, The Kid entered seeing his father soothing his mother by gently stroking her hair as she lay upon him in what appeared to be a loving embrace. The Kid recognized the dysfunction of his parents' dynamics, referring to his parents' relationship as "a freak show". And though enduring physical and emotional abuse himself, within his relationships with bandmates and his intimate relationship with Apollonia, he enacts similar dynamics within his interactions with others.

Safety is a hallmark of flourishing relationships. In the absence of safety, one can have significant difficulties attaching in a healthy manner that leads to the vulnerability required to build and maintain intimate relationships. Due to The Kid's exposure to the volatile interactions of his parents and the aggression his father enacted upon him, his sense of safety appeared never to have been established. His need to assess the family's home for his father's rage prior to entering revealed that his primary need for stable, safe shelter was not available to him. The lack of safety he felt with his caregivers manifested the narrative that he could not trust others globally. With business owners and his bandmates, The Kid questioned their loyalty, feared that people would abandon him, and felt that others did not have his best interests at heart.

Additionally, The Kid struggled with modulating his negative affect in an appropriate manner. When upset, he is found running down hallways offstage only to damage his belongings within the dressing room as a result of an emotional tantrum. When his bandmates confront him on his behavior, rather than engage in a conversation with them directly, The Kid utilizes a puppet that lives in a cone and acts as a ventriloquist to state an evasive response to their concerns. Distancing himself and using the puppet in a displaced manner allows him to remain engaged, yet safe within the conflicted space emotionally. When upset within his intimate relationship with Apollonia, The Kid behaves in a similar fashion to his father, hitting her to the ground, picking her up, and asking that she reassures him that he makes her happy—reenacting the self-described "freak show" of his parents' marital dynamics. The physically abusive interaction that occurs between The Kid and Apollonia invites audiences to witness the beginnings of understanding the sequelae of intergenerational trauma.

24 Living Black (1980–1989)

A final point of consideration: though hurt by The Kid numerous times, Apollonia accepts him for who and where he is in his emotional development. One can wonder regarding Apollonia's exposure to trauma and abuse due to her commitment to The Kid after his assaults on her. The audience is not provided information about Apollonia's past. Rather, she is introduced figuring her way into a hotel room to stay across the street from the club she is interested in performing at. With no additional information, it leaves a great deal of questions where one can be curious as to who she was before arriving in the city and meeting The Kid. However, we understand that she would like to be "helped" by The Kid in developing her singing career. Though warned by Morris (performed by Morris Day) that The Kid is only willing to help himself, Apollonia pursues a working and intimate relationship with him. We also see that her ability to tolerate The Kid's emotionally labile displays is great, where he acts out towards her and she sustains a desire to relate to him. In fact, during one incident where she observes that he is experiencing challenges regulating his anger, she provides him an invitation to "go ahead, hit me".

Concluding, moved by the final musical performance, The Kid and Apollonia reunite with a lack of resolve to their conflictual past, seducing the audience to suppress the assaults that have been seen and collude with the secrecy that trauma motivates. Through entertaining performances that allow all around The Kid to forgive him for past behaviors, the audience tends to do so as well, while leaving with hope for the future of The Kid's and Apollonia's relationship.

Krush Groove (1985)

The musical landscape of the 1980s was one of significant evolution. The expansion of rap and birth of hip hop created a culture that was all-inclusive. There was a musical style featuring a new sound, new artists, fashion equipped with accessories, and dance that accompanied the culture. *Krush Groove* uses the life of producer/manager Russell Simmons and his artists during the budding years of his career. While excitement fluttered with the reception of rap within the community, the reality of a lack of funding sources led the protagonist to make deals with a community loan shark, leaving him looking for ways to return the investment.

The narrative that individuals within the African American community could become successful by hard work and grit was not an unfamiliar tale from decades previously. Pulling oneself up by one's bootstraps was a common notion, yet what happens when the straps of the boots are faulty? The desire to follow one's dreams to become successful took Russell on a journey that required him to find his way through the support of friends and family. *Krush Groove* provides an early behind-the-scenes account of hip hop, business arrangements, and how producers and managers worked with their artists. Exposing the drive required to bring to the public the works of the artist and the expense (emotional and financial) needed to pursue an entrepreneurial venture is also highlighted.

This film also generated support due to the manner that it influenced African Americans within their communities. The culture of African Americans (80s rap and hip hop specifically) was presented on the silver screen where the audience could relate in a communal film experience in the theater. Audiences were shown artists who were familiar and recognizable because they were within the homes of the filmgoer on music videos and the new network Music Television (known as MTV). These artists portrayed shared ideas, customs, and social behaviors of the culture in a manner that was aligned to the experience of those within inner cities while at the same time was mainstream, supporting that this aspect of the African American culture rose to the importance of being shared in the box office.

Krush Groove has a constant theme of the protagonist attempting to find ways to be successful in the music world by amplifying artist talents. Yet, audiences are also exposed to the manner in which individuals viewed themselves, their achievements, ideas about body size, and ways in which they felt about sociopolitical conflicts. Whether it was The Dynamic Three rap group that began to identify themselves as "The Fat Boys" after a vulnerable conversation regarding being authentic about their personal understanding of their physical presentation, or Kurtis Blow rapping about injustices for people of color in America, this film offers individuals the ability to be reflective regarding body perception and the African American rap and hip hop culture.

She's Gotta Have It (1986)

Lee opens with photographs of African Americans, documenting lives lived in New York, with a jazz accompaniment that is sprinkled intermittently throughout the duration of the film. Nola Darling (acted by Tracie Camilla Johns) is presented in an interview-style feature that inquires how she has adopted her beliefs regarding dating and "what makes her tick". Nola is mysterious to others. She lacks interest in exclusive intimate partnership, rejects monogamy, and desires transparent relationships with three men: Mars (performed by Spike Lee), Jamie (acted by Tommy Redmond Hicks), and Greer (acted by John Canada Terrell). To further complicate the matter for her male suitors, she holds a dear relationship with Ava (performed by Cheryl Burr) who is equally interested in helping Nola explore a relationship with her. Nola's understanding of herself allows her to follow her curiosities which leads her to be interested and pursue various connections. However, the men in her life are baffled by her lack of desire for a committed relationship. They scold her for not desiring to marry an individual with financial stabilities and career success, question her regarding what she desires, accuse her of not knowing what she truly wants, and are led to consider that her sexual appetite is a symptom of a sexual addiction where her behaviors are described by one of her suitors as "sick". Despite the assessment of a mental health counselor assuring her that she lacks criteria for a diagnosable condition, these men attempt to analyze her, her motivations, and ultimately why their requests for exclusivity are rejected time and time again.

She's Gotta Have It's title primes the audience for a female lead character who is insatiable in her needs. The title leads one to consider that this character will behave in whatever fashion she must in order to gain what she desires. One must wonder, what is the "it" in the title referring to exactly? She must have a relationship? She must have what she desires without compromise? Sex? An undeniable, unwavering love from others? All of the above?

This film was eye-opening for many in the 1980s, welcoming a view of a woman (written by Spike Lee, who played Mars) who possessed behaviors that were readily observed within male roles historically. The role reversal was present not only in the character of Nola, but also for her male suitors who were pining for her dedicated affection. These characters found themselves lacking understanding of her lack of desire to commit, which led them to provide ultimatums that threatened to terminate the relationship if she did not choose them and only them.

We are able to see the exploration of the various ways one can be attracted to and love one person while being attracted to and loving another in a different way. Nola shows the audience that having a caring, loving relationship with one individual does not have to preclude or minimize the care and love one has for another. Rather, life does not have to equal making a choice that limits one from making another choice. She suggests that an individual can hold and honor the diversity of her partners without sacrificing her affections for others in her life. What is not explicitly stated is that Nola's behaviors are suggestive of a desire of having a polyamorous relationship, a term "coined by Morning Glory Ravenheart Zell around 1990". "Formed from Latin and Greek roots that translate as 'loving many', this word has been adopted" (Easton & Hardy, 1997, p. 8) after the release of this film. These authors continue, "some use it to mean multiple committed live-in relationships, forms of group marriage; others use it as an umbrella word to cover all forms of sex and love and domesticity outside of conventional monogamy" (p. 8). Nola makes each suitor aware of her choices and has the desire for them to connect with one another (as she invites all three to share Thanksgiving with her). However, her male partners struggle to agree to this type of relationship without feuding in competition with one another.

Through Nola's partners' personal accounts, we find that the men in her life actively attempted to understand her behaviors without avail. It was hypothesized that she could not move away from familiar types of men from her neighborhood, that she had unresolved issues with her father, and more. Yet, her account was simple: her love lacked boundaries and being with one person was not what she wanted for her life. In an effort to defend against the rejection and competition that her partners felt between one another, the men in Nola's life employed numerous defense mechanisms to continue in the relationship under her terms. For example, Jamie relied upon reaction formations typically, suggesting that the situation was not as bad as he actually experienced. As an alternative, he anticipated that providing her with time would allow her to come around to his conclusion of monogamy. Similarly, Greer also used reaction formations; however, he tended to rely upon intellectualization implying that Nola was not aware of what she had in him and was foolishly placing the relationship at risk. Mars, on the other hand, related to Nola while primarily suppressing his feelings regarding the situation. When he was no longer able to hold his feelings under the surface, he, as the others, succumbed to the competition that existed amongst her partners. And Nola, remaining optimistic

Living Black (1980–1989)   27

the men would come to accept and craft an agreement with one another, in many ways showed her use of fantastical denial of the impact her decisions had upon the men in her life. Consequently, Nola concludes happy, alone, and firm in her stance of preferring a lack of love over monogamy.

Hollywood Shuffle (1987)

Hollywood Shuffle is a film comprised of a nearly all-African American cast, that through carefully crafted satire highlights the blatant stereotypes found within film using the actors who portray said roles in the industry. The struggle to be cast in films, based upon the countless interested actors in competition for the same roles, creates a scarcity platform that supports a hunger and desperation for any role available in the industry. *Hollywood Shuffle* suggests that the powerful desire to gain employment in the industry means that individuals who are consciously aware of sociopolitical dynamics must call upon the use of higher-order defenses of rationalization, reaction formations, and intellectualizations to cope with the decision to pursue and perpetuate stereotypes of Black people.

Sitting in comedy that pokes fun at the culture, individuals within this film are required to make decisions regarding who they are and the values they will hold. There are questions to answer including: Will one continue to work in positions that do not actualize one's dreams? Will one attempt to reach one's goals despite one's obligations? Will one act in a manner that requires stereotypes to continue about the Black community for work, or will one take a stand despite the consequence(s)? Will I engage my superego in the work I perform? If so, to what extent; to the extent that I reject the roles I work hard to be provided due to my beliefs and protection of the Black community?

Bobby, performed by Robert Townsend, finds with the support of those who care for him that he is asked to confront who he will be and whether he will contribute to the negative ways in which African American individuals are portrayed on screen. In determining whether obtaining the lead role in the film *Jivetime Jimmy's Revenge* directed by three white filmmakers would be right for him, he is interrogated by family, friends, and fellow actors regarding what would be his part in setting negative tones for the African American community. The voices of individuals' thoughts and feelings lent Bobby the ego necessary to contemplate the impact of the behaviors that were scripted for "Jimmy" and the impact it could have upon the Black community. Ultimately, the support Bobby received from his family, including attending the filming of the movie despite having significant reservations regarding the content of the script, illustrated that his family would support his choices regardless of not agreeing with them. In wrestling with his thoughts, Bobby's superego did not allow him to engage in the direction provided by the director to "stick the ass out, bug the eyes out" when instructed that his behaviors needed to appear "more Black". For Bobby, he no longer had the ability to be blind nor close his eyes to the racial dynamics that were being enacted in the service of being an employed actor.

The Color Purple (1988)

The novel *The Color Purple*, by Alice Walker (1982), is a compelling tale that in 1983 earned its author the distinction of being the first African American woman to win a Pulitzer Prize for fiction. The film is one that illustrates the range of love that can exist within the human experience: familial love, romantic love, and, finally, the love for oneself.

Celie is a teenager who finds herself impregnated by her father, involuntarily required to relinquish her children immediately after giving birth, and obligated to marry a sharecropper "Mister". Within this marriage, Celie is debased by her emotionally, physically, and sexually abusive husband. Celie is a timid individual who minimizes herself within every space in which she finds herself, allowing herself to appear nearly nonexistent in a manner which appears to be used as a survival technique. However, she finds that she is able to be most herself in one secured relationship that she has: the relationship with her sister, Nettie.

When her relationship with her sister experiences a forced separation due to Mister's envious rage and vengeance because Nettie will not engage in sexual relations with him, Celie is bereft by her absence and lack of information regarding her whereabouts. Within the years and decades to follow, Celie connects with female figures within her community. She positions herself as a silent observer in most settings, covering the smile she was once told was "ugly" by her father and engaging in a manner that suggests she is unsure of herself and how she belongs in the world. And yet, the women she brings emotionally near treat her with respect, where she is successful in crafting friendships through care, pains, assaults, and abuses that she personally endures and the women in her life also experience by the will of their paramours. It is not until Celie meets Shug, her husband's lover, that she is introduced to a way of understanding herself, as a sexual being who can be a mutual partner in a pleasurable sexual intimate relationship.

The dynamics of power and control is saturated within the fabric of many of the relationships contained in this narrative (Celie and her "father", Mister and Celie, Shug and Mister, Harpo and Ms. Sophia, and Harpo and Squeak, as examples). These relationships are characterized by the exercise of power and control over women, their bodies, their rights, and their liberty to have chosen intimate partners. Power and control dynamics are illustrated in the existing family relations and in the relationship one has by being Black within their southern community. The women are portrayed in a manner where they are managed by the men in their lives and are at the mercy of their treatment towards them (with the exception of Ms. Sophia, who will not stand for such injustices within her home directed towards her, yet endures with loud protest her husband's infidelity. Though, Ms. Sophia is finally silenced by societal rule, imprisoning her in jail for many years and releasing her to a life of servitude with Ms. Millie, a desperate and at times manipulative white woman, for what would be considered today as an assault on a government official). And though Shug could argumentatively be considered a woman in Celie's world who also indulged in independent freedoms as a sensuous juke joint performer, she is bound by the judgment of her father who disowns her for her choices and only reconciles when she is spiritually called to abandon her post at the juke joint and move an entire community in the melodic hollers of "God is Trying to Tell You Something" at the church he pastors.

There is a dependence upon another for one's every need including one's gratitude for one's life, that perpetuates the power one has over the other within the characters of *The Color Purple*. In the summer of 1908 in the South where this film begins, we find that one's emotional captivity is not contained to one's experience within the home; but, rather, these characters face similar physical and emotional enslavements by their community for being an individual of color within America. As a result of these oppressive dynamics, the audience is subjected to being a bystander to perpetual traumas enacted upon these women. The tenacious adversities that characters were required to overcome (i.e. non-consented marital unions, rape, imprisonment, etc.) made visible how living under traumatic circumstances can manifest in individuals living in emotionally defensive spaces for both one's safety and survival. Ultimately what is witnessed in this film is a culmination of violence: intimate partner violence (IPV), family violence ("childhood victimization in the form of observing violence between parents/caregivers or experiencing childhood physical abuse was associated with being the victim or perpetrator of adult IPV", West, 2021, p. 753), historical trauma ("the collective spiritual, psychological, emotional and cognitive distress perpetuated inter-generationally deriving from multiple denigrating experiences originating with slavery and continuing with pattern forms of racism and discrimination", West, 2021, p. 753), structural violence ("Social structural inequalities", West, 2021, p. 754), institutional violence (when one is met with racism, discrimination, or microaggressions at formal agencies and organizations), and cultural violence ("widespread attitudes or beliefs used to justify direct or structural violence, such as prejudices or stereotypes that exist in society which are then internalized by individuals", West, 2021, p. 755 notes from Galtung, 1990).

Within the years that progress, over a forty-year span of time, we see the characters mature. Celie is able to make difficult and brave decisions regarding how she would like to live her life, which requires her to care and depend upon herself in a manner with which she is unfamiliar. She finds that she is not the only woman in these relational dynamics that has a desire to escape, find peace, and pursue a life of personal fulfillment. She is able to, without articulation nor shift in her environment, craft safe places that exist in the protected spaces of her mind created partially by reading found letters from her estranged sister living in Africa withheld by her husband for decades. It was through the promise of her sister's physical safety and fantasized world experience that Celie began to find herself through the pain and was able to begin desiring a future of freedom for herself.

From a varying perspective, the progression of the film depicts the gradual evolution of one's energies focused upon the foundational layer of Maslow's Hierarchy of Needs. At the onset, the characters find themselves scarcely able to access the basic needs of life. Many of the characters experience housing insecurity, a lack of

30 Living Black (1980–1989)

connection to those who are dependable, loving, and safe, and even lack freedom over one's reproduction at the onset of the story. We find at the conclusion of the film the characters arrive to an emotional space of engaging in the highest tier of Maslow's Hierarchy, Self-Actualization. It is within this space that the characters were able to dare to dream of their lives in the absence of a man for their survival.

It should be stated within the recognition of this film that the NAACP protested *The Color Purple*. Specifically, it was suggested that the film was responsible for "sanitizing Alice Walker's themes and her perspectives" coupled with illustrating a "neutralized" version of the lesbian relationship of the main character Celie and Shug. Further, "The African American men—including Mister and the terrorizing father played by Adolph Caesar—often looked like the brutal buck stereotype. The movie was also criticized for being almost too beautiful, not showing the devasting poverty in which the characters lived" (Bogle, 2019, p. 175). Bogle (2019) continued that despite this, "the Color Purple treated its African American women with sensitivity. Rarely had there been close-ups of Black female characters so urgent and so loving. The actresses illuminated the inner conflicts, sorrows and joys of their characters" (p. 175) and highlighted how an emotional fortitude fueled by the love of oneself and support of one's community can provide the self with an opportunity to reposition into greater insight, honesty, and self-actualization.

Colors (1988)

Starring Sean Penn and Robert Duvall as lead characters, *Colors* showcases the Los Angeles Police Department C.R.A.S.H. (Community Resources Against Street Hoodlums 1979–2000) officers working in gang-riddled neighborhoods in downtown LA. With the constant display of police presence and authority surveilling the inner-city streets and alleys of Los Angeles, this film draws upon exploring the definition of community and family, how these systems can be, and how they serve individuals. For those who lack familial ties or have insecure attachments with their family, a gang can provide respect, intimacy, and love that result in a secure relationship with a loyalty that is unwavering—one that individuals are willing to venture their lives upon. Within this film, the display of familial relationships and the consequences of belonging to a gang that included frequent investigations by the police, illegal behaviors, and death by violence are made stark, portraying that there is a desire to use splitting, placing individuals within good or bad classifications, when thinking about the police (inherently good?) and gangs (inherently bad?). However, *Colors* offers the viewer to integrate and conceptualize how individuals can have greater complexity. Officer Hodges' (Robert Duvall) policing behaviors, for example, are questionable. Which is he? Good or bad? Whom does he work to benefit, the police or the gangs? As a result, Officer McGavin (Sean Penn) struggled to understand his police partner. *Colors* suggests that individuals, and people creating communities, are not all good nor are they all bad, yet find themselves living—and some surviving—in between.

Notably, this action film struggled to move on from the frequent stereotypes of men of color. Specifically, as most characters in the film are of color, these characters were cast as supporting artists within the film, providing no lead roles to minority individuals. The roles that were available in this film for those of color included men who displayed well-known stereotypes, further inculcating the implicit messaging that those belonging to Black and brown identities are unsafe and dangerous. The casting of these two police officers was in juxtaposition to the cast of individuals performing characters as gang members, "hoodlums", drug users, and criminals. The few persons of color within the film that did not fall into one of these categories included an ex-gang member and police officers peppered within the scenes. As this film grossed nearly five times its budget this film's exposure was not small in magnitude.

Coming to America (1988)

The long history of the feminist movement is recognized to have originated well before the first documented film. Since then, there have been waves of feminist theory and ideas that have shaped the American culture significantly in influencing how women are positioned and position themselves within the home, workforce, and intimate relationships. In the 1980s, Americans experienced third-wave feminist influences, described as women who wanted both a professional career, as well as to be a wife and mother. Harriet Kimble Wrye wrote of her research on the psychoanalytic perspectives of being a feminist in the twentieth century, "So many of us look back, and recognizing the pressures under which we struggled, wonder how we did what we did and at what price" (Kimble Wrye, 2009, p. 186). These desires came and continue to come at a large cost to one's energy, self-concept, and identity as a woman in America. However, as these desires may have been newly discovered by some women in America, many women of color identified with having a career as well as being a wife and a mother, not out of desires of liberation, but as an obligation to be able to survive within America. For many African American women, these roles were well established prior to the defined feminist waves with less opportunity for flexibility. For instance, working in various positions, one and at times two positions outside of the home, and being a primary caregiver as well as a wife was the understanding. Though, in the 1980s within the African American community, the woman who could present in this capacity successfully was admired, respected, and sought after. And a partnership with such a woman was what Akeem (performed by Eddie Murphy) desired to acquire when he decided to travel to America.

The prince of Zamunda, Akeem is required for his twenty-first birthday to marry Imani (acted by Vanessa Bell), a woman who has been groomed since birth to be his bride. In an effort to be pleasing, she is trained to adopt his interests and follow all commands he provides. Yet, Akeem lacks interest in obtaining a union with a woman that has historically been fitting for a king. Rather, he desires a partner, an individual who has independent thought, is employed, cares for others, and can challenge him intellectually. In his search Akeem embarks on a journey to America. His sojourn is one that many individuals within emerging adulthood make on their path of determining who they are within their identity. Akeem presents in the

32 Living Black (1980–1989)

life phase characterized by separation/individuation that is first observed in early childhood as independence increases. During this time, individuals are supported by their parents in their newly developed differences; whereas, other times, these dissimilarities can lead to significant conflict. Within the film, Akeem is found by his parents (performed by James Earl Jones and Madge Sinclair) in Queens and demanded by his father to return home to marry his chosen bride. When Akeem refuses to return to Africa without Lisa (performed by Shari Headley), the woman he has fallen in love with, his father notes that his behavior does not follow tradition. It is during this moment the parent–child dyad has an opportunity to hold on to set traditions or flex in a manner that supports the child rather than alienating them for growing into their individual selves. When his father justifies his requests to follow the set traditions of Zamunda and wonders who he and his son are to change the standards, Akeem's mother remarks, "I thought you were the king", supporting meeting their son where he is rather than holding rigid boundaries.

There is another aspect of interpersonal dynamics within this film that is typically reduced and suppressed when recalling this film, possibly influenced by the extravagance portrayed both from a romantic light and in terms of visual aesthetics. However, specifically, with Akeem and Lisa's relationship, there is a prolonged act of deception that Akeem performs to gain an opportunity to fall in love with Lisa. In an effort to learn whether Lisa will love him in the absence of considering his princely position, he informs her that in Africa he is a goat herder—and consequently, a "poor man". This concept is mentioned several times as his intent is for her to be under a false pretense while he is learning whether she could love someone with a lack of financial security. One may wonder, why was there a test? Astutely, when Lisa is asked to accept his marriage proposal, she notes that due to his disguise, she does not know who he is. What is not shown in the film is what is required of Lisa to arrive in Africa and marry Akeem. What was her process of understanding his deception? How did she arrive to a place of feeling that additional dishonest interactions would not occur or she would be willing to tolerate them? How did she decide to "take a chance" after all and commit to a lifetime with Akeem? These areas of the film remain a mystery and offer the audience the use of creative liberties to fill in or suppress the importance of these factors when beginning a marital union. This film in its current presentation illustrated that in Hollywood, these aspects of human relationships held less consequence, yet in the real world they may be of benefit to explore.

Do the Right Thing (1989)

The 1980s decade of African American film was capped with many evocative films. For instance, *Tap* (1989), *Harlem Nights* (1989), and *Glory* (1989) created a range of affect in audiences. Most offered hope that change can shift oppressive states of mind, there can be hope of rehabilitation, hope of new beginnings, and hope for global freedom. *Do the Right Thing*, written and directed by Spike Lee, illustrated that prior to hope arriving, there are events that occur that can include acts of discussion, negotiation, lack of understanding, resistance, and soul-experienced frustration that result in both death and new opportunities for living while exasperated.

Do the Right Thing is set in Brooklyn on the hottest day of the summer. Mookie (performed by Spike Lee) is a twenty-five year old male employed as a pizza deliverer for Sal's Pizzeria, an Italian American establishment in the heart of an African American community. Mookie's personal world includes his sister Jade (acted by Joie Lee), his son Hector, and girlfriend Tina (acted by Rosie Perez). Additionally, Mookie is familiar with neighborhood residents, the local alcoholic Da Mayor (performed by Ossie Davis), the maternal figure that watches the neighborhood from her stoop (Mother Sister acted by Ruby Dee), Radio Raheem (performed by Bill Nunn) who walks the neighborhood with his boombox that blares "Fight The Power", Smiley (acted by Roger Guenveur Smith) who is a developmentally delayed individual, and Buggin Out (performed by Giancarlo Esposito), a friend of Mookie's. His professional world involves Sal, the owner of the pizzeria (Danny Aiello), and Sal's two sons Pino (acted by John Turturro) and Vito (performed by Richard Edson). Mookie experiences antagonizing interactions with Pino based upon racial biases yet is always met with kindness from Vito. When it is noted by Buggin Out that Sal conducts business in a Black neighborhood and the success of the shop is due to Black patrons, it is questioned why his wall of fame does not include African American people, rather it is decorated with only Italian Americans. Sal resists, reminding Buggin Out that it is his establishment and if there is desire for a different experience, they should pursue opening their own business with a wall of fame to reflect that desire. Later, Buggin Out, Radio Raheem, and Smiley return demanding that the wall becomes inclusive; Sal refers to Buggin Out as a "nigger" and, in a fit of rage, takes a bat to Radio Raheem's boombox. As a result, a physical altercation ensues, police become involved, and Radio Raheem is restrained and killed by strangulation by a police officer. Sal's Pizzeria becomes engulfed in flames by protest and left in ashes.

Do the Right Thing illustrates for audiences how an ordinary day can lead to a grieving night when individuals feel that they lack a voice to be heard and, when attempting to advocate, experience disrespect. Dr. Martin Luther King, Jr. stated, "A riot is the language of the unheard" (1966)—a fitting statement for this film. Dr. Lauren Duncan, professor at Smith College, describes that there are "movements of crisis and movements of conscience. In times of crisis, immediate reaction to maybe a killing or some sort of violence, people may react to what just happened in a disorganized way without any articulated political analysis of what's going on." She continues, "but then you have crisis of conscience, which tends to happen in times where basic human needs are met and people are agitating for rights" (Duncan, 2020). On this evening in Brooklyn, a movement of conscience occurs where Buggin Out is clear regarding what the desire is for Sal's Pizzeria and there is a clear articulation of the political influence of the situation. And though the riot is a crisis in itself, it is the result of a member of the community being able to label the dynamics in his community that was imbued by racism.

34   Living Black (1980–1989)

This film shows the complexity of human relations in a nuanced way. On one hand it challenges the audience to conceptualize what it must be like to live within a community and support a business while feeling that your support is expected, yet be taken for granted and disrespected. On the other hand, it welcomes ponderance into what it must be like to have built a business in the manner you envisioned, only to have patrons express their disapproval of your choices. The negotiation between what one desires and what the community requires is called into question. Does a privately owned business whose survival depends on the community's patronage have a responsibility to its community other than to provide the agreed-upon service of deliverable good(s)? Does a business have the obligation to respond to the callings of the community or does it maintain its independence? How much is a business the community's and how much of it is the private owner's?

Sal perceives that his pizzeria is a lone business within the community and a place of pride for his family and his heritage. He and his sons lack awareness of the collective unconscious where the community's thoughts, desires, and opinions comprise the environment in which Sal has chosen to have a business operation. Rather, Sal minimizes his personal and business's impact on his community by dismissing the request of including historical images within his restaurant. Were he to include the history of persons belonging to the community he serves, his patrons would feel recognized and respected in his establishment. Choosing not to honor his patrons' history in his establishment speaks volumes about his perspective of the individuals who make his professional self and financial lifestyle possible.

Further, Sal's Pizzeria serves as a nutritional source for this community. His establishment is the local pizzeria offering food to those who desire it. Though what he delivers is a friendly veneer, the depths of how he engages in the community are riddled with prejudice, honored stereotypes, and racism. As the community consume what Sal creates, bakes in an oven, and has delivered to their home, the community also ingest subconsciously, and some more consciously, the thoughts and feelings held by those employed at the shop. A select few (i.e. Buggin Out and Radio Raheem) soon realize that what Sal is selling has the potential to be destructive to one's self-esteem, self-respect, and community as a whole.

Do the Right Thing was a successful film critically and commercially while holding its position for decades thereafter. It has been a production that has received accolades of the highest esteem and was noted as "culturally, historically, or aesthetically significant" by the Library of Congress in 1999. It remains in use today for conversations to be had regarding race, ethnicity, and protest; and, unfortunately, to reveal the similarities this fictional film of 1989 reflects in Americans' sociopolitical world today.

Harlem Nights (1989)

The perceptions that we hold for characters and the feelings that are elicited through film can be a unique experience. With powerful storytelling, many times we find that we have strong feelings and reactions towards the characters that are in films.

These feelings allow the audience to experience the range of feelings of aligning, becoming upset, disappointed, and even idealizing the characters and what they represent. *Harlem Nights* is similar to other gangster stories that begin in 1918 and continue into the 1930s era. Live jazz bands, women in flapper attire, and men in three piece suits topped with hats prime the audience in locating the scene in 1930s Harlem. The protagonists, Sugar Ray and Quick, are individuals crafted with layers that elicit visceral reactions to their characters, their choices, decisions, and behaviors.

Within Harlem in 1918, Sugar Ray, performed by Richard Prior, is a small business owner who hosts a speakeasy of gambling in his basement. A young Vernest Brown (Desi Arnez Hines II) enters as an errand runner and is met with a hostile gambler who lost their funds on a bet after noting their dislike for children and their belief in children being bad luck. When the angry gambler threatens Sugar Ray with a switchblade for his money to be returned and threatens the life of Vernest, Vernest shoots the man with a gun. Due to his rapid response to the situation, Vernest is thereafter referred to as "Quick" as an adult (acted by Eddie Murphy). When Sugar Ray learns that Quick is an orphan, he takes him into his guardianship and employs him until his adult years.

Due to the success of Sugar Ray's establishment, a local white gangster, Bugsy Calhoune (performed by Michael Lerner), desires a financial profit from his earnings. As a result, he sends an enforcer and Ms. Dominique LaRue (Jasmine Guy), Calhoune's mistress, to examine his facilities. When it is found that his establishment is profitable, Calhoune sends a police officer, Sergeant Phil Cantone (Danny Aiello), to threaten to close his business. In response, Sugar Ray decides to close his business, yet he would like to ensure that he and all who work for him are financially cared for. Within an elaborate gambling plan on a boxing match, Sugar Ray and his friends are able to escape Mr. Calhoune's advances, yet must say goodbye to Harlem and reestablish themselves elsewhere.

This film has fertile character and theme development present. These characters in their richness engage in a complex tale of engaging in illegal activities of gambling and killing while having a humanity and loyalty to those with whom they have spent a lifetime in the business. And yet, for those who screen this film, one finds oneself rooting for Sugar Ray, his employees, and his dear friends who are also equally engaged in illegal activities of gambling, prostitution, murder, and the like. With the goal of evading paying Mr. Calhoune, the audience is made aware that Sugar Ray has intentions of continuing his illegal activities, only in a different part of the United States. However, positive regard is held for these characters. This feeling allows one to disavow (deny by splitting off unacceptable aspects of one's environment) the reality and impact of Sugar Ray's plans. Acknowledging that their successful flight from Harlem, physical and financial security, and ability to relocate will not only be a journey into the sunset on a late Harlem night, but rather a plan riddled with a future of legal indiscretions and murders of others in the place they decide to settle, invites one to reconsider one's feelings towards the characters, maybe? Because characters are shown in their fullness, where one character does not

36 Living Black (1980–1989)

hold only one negative attribute, it influences how one responds to these characters with greater understanding of who they are and consequently with greater grace. For example, we find Sugar Ray has an illegal gambling business, yet is kind with his employees and takes full guardianship of a child he only meets moments earlier, suggesting there is an altruistic kindness to this man who also stands by when people are murdered within his presence and shows no remorse. Being exposed to the various characteristics of Sugar Ray allows space to be made to conceptualize the character globally rather than holding only one aspect of his personality.

Additionally, *Harlem Nights* offers a story told of the early 1900s that included people of color as the lead and primary persons within the film. Historically, films that depicted this time period either were devoid of the presence of individuals of color or placed POC within limited roles. *Harlem Nights* featuring the lives of African Americans in Harlem showcases the presence of people of color in a manner that did not place them in roles of servitude to white people, rather as profitable racketeers that white fellow criminals sought after. This film shows that throughout history African Americans have been able to build institutions that are sustainable and are equally successful players in America, even in the illegal underbellies found in the basements of candy stores at Sugar Ray's.

Legacy Films

Each decade of cinema offers audiences the opportunity to return to the past for inspiration that pays homage to our ancestors. These stories, both fiction and nonfiction, are diverse, providing audiences newly held information and enabling them to leave with an education that the film highlights. Within this chapter we will consider the films *School Daze* (1988), *Lean on Me* (1989), *Tap* (1989), and *Glory* (1989). To add to the richness of the exploration of the film *School Daze*, an intimate virtual focus group of Black fraternity members and individual interviews with Black sorority members across African American Greek organizations were held at the close of 2023 and beginning of 2024 to glean personal accounts regarding how *School Daze* was experienced in the 1980s as a viewer and the impact, if any, the film had upon their life decisions and lived experience.

School Daze (1988)

College years are ripe with new experiences, and the development of friendships and bonds that can last a lifetime. Within the years of emerging adulthood, critical life realizations about the world and the self are occurring. During this stimulating life phase, interpersonal connections generated within the process of engaging with others who share values and ideals while pledging to a life of service in the African American community are what many find in pursuing Greek life. *School Daze* (1988), Spike Lee's second feature within the 1980s, depicts a version of individuals' experience(s) becoming and belonging to African American Greek organizations upon a fictional Historical Black College campus in the 1980s.

Half Pint, performed by Spike Lee, is on line to cross to become a member of Gamma Phi Gamma fraternity. He along with his line brothers engage in numerous activities upon the request of their big brothers for six weeks of demonstrating their commitment, determination, and perseverance to the organization, their brothers, and to themselves. Half Pint's big brother, Julian, or "Big Brother Almighty" (acted by Giancarlo Esposito), leads the pledges while navigating an ongoing conflictual relationship with Dap (performed by Laurence Fishburne), a social activist on campus engaged in demonstrations to bring awareness to the apartheid in South Africa. Julian's girlfriend is also a member within the Greek community, as a member of the Gamma Rays that are historically of lighter skin tones with long hair. She and her *sisters* engage in conflictual exchanges with non-Greek women who possess darker skin tones and natural hairstyles, a residue of internalized colonized perspectives of what is "right", "beauty", and "acceptable". [Whether the Gamma Rays were a sorority or sweethearts to Gamma Phi is debatable based upon interpretation. "I saw them as a sorority, not as the sweethearts. Yes, they were supportive of the fraternity", (Interviewee F) shared. "They didn't seem to have their own foundation, rather they were fueled by what was being asked by the fraternity. In the sorority, I never felt that I had to be validated by a fraternity. As a sweetheart, your job is to help the pledgees out", (Interviewee G) added.]

Within a small focus group with members of various fraternities, it was noted one "requires fortitude, perseverance, sticktoitiveness, and heart" (Interviewee D) to successfully cross into Greek life. Given the number of conflicts presented to one during pledging, what keeps people desiring and motivated to become members? The conceptualization of the collective rather than the individual self is examined with the goal "We are stronger as a unit" (Interviewee A). Within a subsequent interview with a sorority member, she reported, "You are synchronized in the process of pledging. You are learning to work as one, like when you see them all sleeping together on line" (Interviewee G). And, with equal importance, Interviewee H described, "I could feel it now. The love, the enthusiasm, the uplifting in that room…I was like this is for me".

Universities hold numerous micro-cultures upon the campus. Some cultures are comprised of members within Greek life, and though *School Daze* suggests that organizations exist in the presence of conflict with one another, most times collaborations amongst members of all Greek organizations exist for the benefit of the whole community. "When lines came out, people cheered people on" (Interviewee F). "There is the family you are born into and the family that you choose" (Interviewee B). In choosing to become a member of a Greek organization in the African American community, it is prided that one is making a lifelong commitment to the brother- or sisterhood coupled with a dedication to service within the African American community. As a result, it may not be surprising that "most civil rights leaders are affiliated with a Greek organization", as Interviewee A stated.

For many individuals, the film *School Daze* has served and continues to serve as a cultural educational resource introducing one to the possibilities of Greek life, especially when one is the first person within their family to matriculate within

38　Living Black (1980–1989)

university or has had limited exposure of engaging in Black communities. Being exposed to the entertainment, laughter, and intellectual and social stimulations of college coupled with a sister- and brotherhood that offers eternal support revealed that furthering one's education at a Historically Black College and University (HBCU) was more than an academic enhancing experience. Rather, higher learning was a personal life-changing evolution for learning who one is, one's values, and at what costs one will uphold these ideals. "School Daze opened my eyes to that there is a different college experience that I didn't know about. There is a whole other life that I didn't know about. Seeing it, I was like, I would like that" (Interviewee H).

Further, one can also glean a greater message from *School Daze*. The act and importance of loving oneself and the challenge of loving others is a dynamic consistently viewed throughout the film. Exchanges made through song and dance of women making demeaning comments regarding phenotypes illustrating self-hate within race, showing the love of another and how it can compromise one's love and respect for oneself as depicted with Jane and Julian at the conclusion of the film, and, opposing, how one can advocate and care for self as witnessed in an exchange with Dap and his love interest Kyme (performed by Rachel Meadows) are also weaved within this film:

> People do feed into this. Lack of self-worth. Comes from a system of white supremacy that has been imposed onto us and how self-destructive they are. We have to wake up and do better. When your self-worth has been etched in these painful fabrics, these conflicting messages, trying to reconstruct and heal the value system in our community coming from almost 400 years of trauma, and people lacking awareness that this is trauma and instead feeling that it is a way to be valued was in the movie.
>
> (Interviewee G).

Though considered an iconic, groundbreaking film for its time, within the African American community this film has also equally received criticism. Audiences are left to wonder regarding the omissions of a number of positive aspects that membership in Greek organizations holds while other aspects such as stepping and pledging are highlighted:

> The pledging process, there were some misconceptions. It trivialized the process to some degree. This is something that I would not mock; something that is so sacred. It is an intense learning process. You are learning 100 years of history. People see how capable they are of learning a lot in a very short amount of time.
>
> (Interviewee G).

"The message for me was there were a lot of stereotypes; this is not real life, this is entertainment. It was not my experience at a HBCU campus" (Interviewee H). It is "understood that the dramatic events were for the mass public and for entertainment value" (Interviewee E) and show the "antithesis of what the fraternity stands for" (Interviewee E). Individuals noted that there was a longing for depictions of members being active within the African American community providing service, and persons unifying and collaborating with university and state leadership as well as with other Greek organizations:

> This film suggested that Greeks cannot be conscious. Being Greek meant that you were not in touch with Blackness and was only interested in gallivanting with women. It doesn't show that Greeks tended to lead movements that were deemed conscious at the time and continue to work in these areas today.
>
> (Interviewee D).

A sorority member added that additional aspects wished to have been portrayed included, "we have these rich systems in our communities that are resilient that cultivate healing with sisterhood and brotherhood and we can create organizations that help our communities" (Interviewee G).

Further, as with many films of this time, characters were crafted to hold one major identity, as supported by the character Dap who embodies for the audience social consciousness. He finds himself in resistance with members of his collegial cohort, with members of Greek life, and with the university leadership. Within a brief scene of him and his friends leaving campus, he is confronted by locals who declare that their education will deem them still as a "nigger" after commencement, and they were no better than those without a college education. One explores whether it is wrong to desire an education, to become Greek, to want more. Bravely, Dap closes the physical gap between he and Leeds (acted by Samuel Jackson) and states, "You are not niggers", showing him that he is seen for who he is, that he is so much more than he is aware. Dap provides him an invitation to esteem himself in a manner that is not dictated by others, but managed on his own accord. Being "woke" calls Dap at the conclusion of the film to exit his dorm hall, ring the yard bell, and yell, "Wake up!" to all who come to witness his demonstration of frustration. And though this film cleverly called audiences into theaters to see students step, dance, and view college life, possibly for the first time, this film of social awareness and social consciousness remains imprinted upon audiences 35 years in its wake generating active conversation and young adult memories.

Glory (1989)

The film *Glory* provides a window into the struggles of our African American ancestors who dedicated a portion of their lives to the hope of liberation in the United States. Set during the Civil War, men of color were provided the opportunity to contribute to the fight for freedom against the Southern confederacy. *Glory* documents from letters of Robert Gould Shaw, a reluctant leader of the famous 54th Massachusetts Infantry, his experience sculpting African American men into soldiers. In doing so, the soldiers and Shaw became one of the first African American

40 Living Black (1980–1989)

regiments in the Civil War Union Army. This dramatic narrative introduces the lives of various characters with varying pasts, that depict the conflicts that live intra- and interracially within African American people of yesterday and today. This film also highlights the power of unifying on agreed-upon beliefs and desires.

Private Trip (performed by Denzel Washington) is introduced as an independent man with a way of creating agitation amongst others. Entering the tent with fellow soldiers Sgt. Maj. John Rawlins (acted by Morgan Freeman), Cpl. Thomas Searles (acted by Andre Braugher), and Pvt. Jupiter Sharts (acted by Jihmi Kennedy), Private Trip observed the behaviors of the African American soldiers—and frequently uninvitedly made comment on their behavior as problematic and a product of systemic racism. Particularly, Private Trip frequently noted when behavior appeared to "please the white man" or "please the master", causing individuals to contemplate their behavior. Consequently, his presentation caused discomfort in interpersonal exchanges and appeared to engender feelings of shame in his counterparts.

And yet, there were many sides to Private Trip. As he described, his situation prior to enlisting in the Army was as a "runaway" slave with a lack of family ties. He shared that he was accustomed to being on his own, with everything, including his life, to lose. However, when he, as well as the other soldiers, found grim provisions provided and required new shoes due to bleeding weathered feet, he was the only soldier with an audacious character to leave bravely in search of what was needed despite his concerns of being caught and punished. When he was found going against orders, the risk for taking care of himself and his needs resulted in the lashing of leather straps upon his back, which was significantly marred with scars from prior lashings in his life.

Possibly Private Trip's time alone, in constant survival mode, made it difficult for him to connect to others readily without provocation. However, following time spent with his cohort, nearing the conclusion of the film, Private Trip understood his relationship with his peers had changed. Once confiding of his lack of family, Private Trip shares caged words behind his tears, "I love the 54th", a meaningful acknowledgment of the brother bonds crafted during their training and battle together. Though there is not always a happy ending when one is recounting times of battle and war, if one pauses the film at this moment, we are able to see that the time with brothers provided the soldiers with pride and comradery and for Private Trip, and for many other soldiers of today, a family.

Lean on Me (1989)

Inner cities of America in the 1980s within many states were struggling. Low socioeconomic conditions coupled with the crack cocaine epidemic riddled residents and led to inherently impoverished places across the country. One institution hit the hardest was public city schools. The film *Lean on Me* (1989) shares a story of a local high school, Eastside High, within Paterson, New Jersey, experiencing the results of this crisis.

At the onset, we find Eastside High School on its last legs. The students matriculating appear to lack morale or motivation and are constantly exposed to the minimum. Competitive classes are not offered to students for fear they cannot manage the rigors of the courses. This doubt is not unfounded; rather, the new principal, Mr. Joe Clark (performed by Morgan Freeman), is required to increase the number of students able to pass statewide basic academic benchmarks. Though this was historically a thriving school, both drug and gang violence made for unsafe conditions for both students and teacher/administrators alike. Thus, when Mr. Clark returns (as he is a former teacher at the school and discontinued his tenure due to budget cuts), the school, including students, administrators, and parents, experience a great deal of turbulence to cope with the changes he suggests to transition the school.

Taking on the task to turn a sinking school around to soar was a significant undertaking. After a careful assessment of the school to become familiar with its functions (learning how it breathes and lives), Mr. Clark implemented a system that was highly structured. He found that the school was in chaos, lacked structure and effective leadership, and was not meeting the needs of the students or staff. When speaking with his colleagues, the educators at the school, he understood apathy was a cancer within the fabric of the morale metastasizing at an alarming rate rendering most of the educators paralyzed to teach. Most persons in the school appeared to be in survival mode: arrive, attend, and leave safely. Educating appeared low on the list to aspire towards, as most individuals within this space witnessed traumatic events and worked within a place that constantly felt unsafe. Yet, apathy was only a symptom of the problem.

Students matriculating at Eastside High experienced a similar dynamic in and outside of school. They too approached life in survival mode due to exposure to poverty, housing insecurity, and lack of parental supports. In turn, they arrived to the school famished emotionally and unable to attend to the education provided. The students approached the learning environment enacting the emotions that accompany living in survival and displaying their internal experience of anger, rage, and disappointment through fighting and disengagement. Violence within the walls of Eastside High was uncontainable, where both students and teachers were all at risk of physical harm. With all parties focused upon managing what the day would bring and the health of the school, all who were involved used the majority of their energies to maintain being physically present in a protective stance rather than one open to learning and development.

The poster of this film powerfully depicts Mr. Clark leaning over four adolescent boys pointing his finger, with hand on hip appearing as an authority for students. Mr. Clark entered roaring in a manner that took an authoritarian approach to his leader style with a community of students and administrators with an insecure attachment style. He created rules, and if not followed exactly, little negotiation was made to accommodate others' thoughts and ideas. There was a focus on making the environment safe for academic growth and a requirement of students who lacked

42 Living Black (1980–1989)

investment in learning to leave the premises. Radically, Mr. Clark demanded locking the doors to the school against legal fire laws to ensure the environment upheld the basic need of safety of the students and staff once a student was brutally assaulted and stabbed within the cafeteria by a student earlier expelled from the school. With a strong conviction that there would be no compromises to the standards that he would make for the school, some readily embraced this shift and began to engage by participating in community events (i.e. study sessions, beautifying the school), whereas others resisted the transition declaring that they did not require parenting, and, specifically, not his type of parenting. Given the community's insecure attachment, there was a great mistrust of Mr. Clark's approach and intentions; while some were anxious around him, others were avoidant of him. Mr. Clark's convictions provided him "with a personal level of comfort despite volatile environments and conflicts" that arose around him (Marshall Woods, 2018, p. 69). "When peers and/ or authorities challenge one's convictions" (Marshall Woods, 2018, p. 69), "the strength of belief" (Pianalto, 2011, p. 382) tends to become increasingly inflexible and held with greater tenacity. When teachers verbally challenged Mr. Clark, they were temporarily dismissed from duty with the hope they would return with a different understanding. Parents passionately protested his approach and ultimately had him arrested (for locking the doors of the school).

Despite the number of challenges and protests, both literally and figuratively, it became clear that his convictions reflected the passion he had for Eastside High and the community. As a result, Mr. Clark was portrayed in the film as a father figure to many. Students began to come to him with complaints they had, in particular desiring access to classes regardless of their gender and advanced coursework. During times of housing insecurity, teenage pregnancy, parental substance use, and parent–child discord, Mr. Clark was present with a listening ear and provided personal assistance and community resources. Within this school, Mr. Clark created a family—a unit that he would do anything for and they would do anything for him. As people began to work with him, he was challenged to loosen the reins of power and control, reassess, and acknowledge that he had supports behind him, and he and the school were no longer independently navigating the space, but were a collective working towards the same goals. At this time, he began to shift his parental style from authoritarian to an authoritative figure showing greater collaboration and displaying open communication while continuing to set clear rules and boundaries. Mr. Clark began to solve issues with others, and openly communicated with his colleagues while he continued to provide clearly set rules and expectations.

Tap (1989)

The name of this film ensures that the audience interested would receive exactly what they desired, tap performances from many of the most famous tappers alive at the time. Gregory Hines, Sammy Davis Jr., Savon Glover, Howard "Sandman" Sims, Suzzanne Douglas, Jimmy Slyde, Harold Nicholas, and other legends grace the screen with tap routines that highlight the extraordinary talent of each individual artist and the impressive collective body of work created and refined for over a century and a half. With history lessons sprinkled into the narrative through comedy and conflicts, if the world of tap is what the audience desired, this film delivers in scores.

Closely embraced with the art of tap is the story of Max (performed by Gregory Hines), who is on a road of rehabilitation. Max is introduced in Sing Sing Correctional Facility practicing tap within his small cell at night. At the risk of upsetting and disturbing his neighboring inmates, Max is unrelenting until he concludes his practice. When released from prison, he returns to his home neighborhood desiring to engage in his talents and reconnect to his familial culture of dance, though continues to hold fears of being unsuccessful and financially unable. Consequently, Max has decisions to make of whether he will pursue dance as a career or return to a life of theft with his unsavory colleagues.

When one has experienced trauma, we have grown to understand that the process of healing is not an individual experience, rather a communal one (Unger, 2013). Environments need to be amenable for the person to access assistance and support their stage(s) of healing. Due to Max's decision to return to his childhood neighborhood, he allowed himself the opportunity to return to a place where he received support to be his authentic self. We find that each time Max behaves in a manner that is not a reflection of how he understands himself, conflict arises within him and he expresses his negative feelings by acting out aggressively. This behavior is observed several times where Max pursues returning to a life of crime when he feels discouraged, breaks dishes purposefully at his place of employment obtained at the onset of his release from prison when he feels annoyed, frustrated, and possibly bored and disappointed, and assaults the director of a Broadway show when feeling disrespected. Max is created as a character that is easily agitated by his environment and has difficulty respecting rules and boundaries that feel unnecessary to him to observe. He is a character whose reactions manifest in unmodulated anger displays, yet he has the capacity to be gentle and loving to others. As a result, Max has a loyal support network despite the countless ways that he disappoints them; whereas he holds a similar fierce loyalty to performing tap with integrity.

Tap suggests connection is the road of rehabilitation. Connection is the cure. Regaining a sense of community with the legends of yesterday and connecting with and rekindling a past love all while actualizing his personal talents lead Max to be a man with little wanting.

3

Death and Rebirth to Evolution (1990–1999)

African American films continued to gain major traction in theaters by the close of 1989. As a response to the interest audiences had in the work, the number of films greenlit for mainstream viewing more than doubled during the decade that followed. "...SO many doors began to open for Black actors. Hollywood was finally gaining the confidence to invest in untapped Black potential allowing for what I often call The Golden Years of Black Hollywood", Jada Pinkett Smith articulated in her book *Worthy* (2023, p. 134). Specifically, "a new crop of African American filmmakers, both independent and as studio directors, invigorated the decade with a fresh perspective and style" (Bogle, 2019, p. 188). Comedy remained a staple in African American films of the 1980s that depicted struggles and resulted in both personal triumphs and interpersonal success. In comparison, the 1990s offered dramatic tales, many of them fictional, that sobered the souls of viewers. Cinematic works of the 1990s highlighted how the African American community had difficulty moving beyond the basic need of survival through love stories and dramas. Though characters were depicted as those who could overcome one's circumstances, the price of doing so, most times, involved enduring horrific traumatic experiences. Audiences were challenged to consider when happy endings exist; they may occur after one has experienced significant hardship, pain, and loss often as a consequence of perpetual hopelessness found within stagnant communities riddled with violence. For those who managed to escape the landscape of violence, poverty, and desperation for a different lifestyle, the inertia of libidinal drives and a fight for life in the face of chronic despair had a profound presence on this decade of film work.

John Singleton, influenced by the earlier works of filmmakers such as Spike Lee, provided significant narratives of African Americans living in the 1990s. With films such as *Boyz N The Hood* (1991), *Poetic Justice* (1993), and *Higher Learning* (1995) we were able to have a ticket to his desire to "be a part of a revolution, a new wave of African American filmmaking" (Singleton, 2019, p. x). While toying with showing the tension between the death instinct within African American communities and the libidinal drives of individual characters within circumstances that include family discord and societal prejudices, we find films that are complex, yet which educate us regarding lived environments, the successful and unsuccessful

DOI: 10.4324/9781003399902-4

use of defense mechanisms, and aspects of resilience possessed by individuals. These films depict individuals of varying developmental stages that navigate the Freudian death instinct of being of color in America and use varying storytelling platforms that include drama, tragedy, and comedy to demonstrate what aspects of Blackness in the US can be for one's life.

Making space and naming the dynamics found in African American communities that include systemic racism and colonized currents that run through the waves of the African American's experience were amplified. As a result, films such as *Menace II Society* (1993), *Boyz N the Hood* (1991), *Set It Off* (1996), *Clockers* (1995), and others illustrated the impact the community has upon one's life, motivations, and hope. When one's energies are primarily used for survival, the difficulty to conceive "different" (for better or for worse) in life is a challenge. For those who desire something other than what is experienced, there is a restlessness that is characterized by frustration with one's present circumstances. *Boyz N The Hood* (1991), *What's Love Got To Do With It* (1993), and *Jason's Lyric* (1994) for example demonstrate how individuals can utilize such restlessness in desire for different circumstances within their home and local community, whereas *Dead Presidents* (1995) placed light on the desire for a different relationship with communal and government support that was lacking in homage to the 1970s experience of veterans. Within these films, many suggest that for those who survive and are able to find opportunities to explore new ways of existing, there is a death that occurs in various forms and a rebirth to evolution (*Boyz N The Hood*, 1991; *The Five Heartbeats*, 1991; *Juice*, 1992; *Clockers*, 1994; *Higher Learning*, 1995; *Set It Off*, 1996).

Trauma

Films in the 1990s offered narratives to audiences that highlighted the chronic and acute trauma that is experienced within some African American communities. Films such as *Boyz N The Hood* (1991), *Juice* (1992), *Poetic Justice* (1993), *Menace II Society* (1993), *Above the Rim* (1994), *Jason's Lyric* (1994), *Clockers* (1995), *Dead Presidents* (1995), and *Set It Off* (1996) became platforms to view how others lived, survived, and managed exposures to traumatic events within their lives. Many of these films documented within fictional stories youth, their perspectives, conflicts faced, and how equipped or ill-equipped they were to cope with life's circumstances. Particularly, the impacts that crew and gang involvement, gun violence, illegal drug distribution, theft, and assault can have upon a person's psyche and behaviors were highlighted. Additionally, childhood exposure to domestic violence and substance abuse while attempting to determine how to be loyal to loved ones engaged in illegal behaviors when wanting opportunities for a different life were also frequent conflicts depicted. Suggesting that these experiences result in trauma for individuals involved, these cinematic works graphically support the impact traumatic events can have upon a person. Specifically, these narratives illustrated that once one has experienced a traumatic event, for some, symptoms of emotional distress occur immediately and acutely, and for others, reactions from

46 Death and Rebirth to Evolution (1990–1999)

traumatic events linger within the fabric of who a person becomes and are expressed continuously in a manner that struggles to dissipate with time. These symptoms are portrayed accurately, showing that trauma can have a long-lasting impression on one's perspective on life and how one navigates the world after exposure.

As an alternative to examining each film in detail independently, utilizing the ability to understand a series of nine films as a collective to conceptualize the sequelae of trauma is described below. The Diagnostic and Statistical Manual of Mental Disorders, Fifth Edition, Text Revision (DSM-V-TR) provides a number of criteria that are present to consider the diagnosis of Post-Traumatic Stress Disorder (PTSD) to understand an individual's presentation. Within these films we are able to follow characters who have experiences that make them vulnerable to the post-traumatic symptoms that they possess. The following films are used to highlight such criteria, offering visuals of symptom presentation and a greater understanding of the character and theme development found within the films: *Boyz N The Hood* (1991), *Juice* (1992), *Poetic Justice* (1993), *Menace II Society* (1993), *Above the Rim* (1994), *Jason's Lyric* (1994), *Clockers* (1995), *Dead Presidents* (1995), and *Set It Off* (1996). Though it remains encouraged to screen each film prior to reading to glean the greatest insight, it is necessary to offer a warning of the violent content these films contain and the emotional consequences of viewing nine films of this content in succession. As part of a filmmaker's charge is to elucidate for audiences the realities of the lived experience, they may not hold the ethical responsibility of do no harm as psychologists are required to. Consequently, it is encouraged to remain kind to your internal being in the manner which works best for you while viewing.

> **Criterion A: Exposure to actual or threatened death, serious injury or sexual violence by directly experiencing the traumatic event(s), witnessing, in person, the event(s) as it occurred to others, learning that the traumatic event(s) occurred to a close family member or close friend. In cases of actual or threatened death of a family member or friend, the event(s) must have been violent or accidental.**

Contained in these dramatic narratives are varying stories of how traumatic events can occur for individuals. For example, within the film *Boyz N The Hood* (1991), each character experiences a sense of unsafety in a manner that threatens their physical integrity. They find that living in the "hood" makes them vulnerable to altercations with others and drive-by shootings that cause them to quickly cower to the ground in hopes that they find themselves fully intact, without injury and alive. When these events are not happening, rather than have an opportunity to emotionally recover, they are reminded of being trapped in the ever-present violence by hearing the rotors and seeing the shining lights overhead from helicopters surveilling the location for individuals allegedly involved in illegal activities. Such uncertainty regarding whether one will survive the day, or even the next few hours, and constant reminders that one lives in an environment of violence lead the community to be in a perpetual state of crisis.

Within the film *Juice* (1992), the characters orchestrate a situation that becomes the source of their traumatic experiences beginning with performing an armed robbery, where one of the assailants purposefully shoots the store clerk, forever changing the dynamics within the friendship group.

In the film *Poetic Justice* (1993), Justice (performed by Janet Jackson) witnesses her boyfriend's murder as they sit in the car at a drive-in theater on a date. This first scene of the film sets the stage for the manner in which we understand Justice through the duration of the film.

Additionally, the protagonist, Caine (acted by Tyrin Turner), in the film *Menace II Society* (1993), is raised observing the violent murderous interpersonal exchanges of his father and witnessing his mother's substance abuse, which significantly influences his behavioral and psychological presentation.

Similarly, within the films *Above the Rim* (1994) and *Jason's Lyric* (1994), it is immediately learned that a trauma occurred: in the former, the lead Shep (performed by Leon) loses his friend by falling out of a window of a building when unable to stop his momentum after jumping to reach the highest point on a basketball hoop; and in the latter, when the lead, Jason (performed by Allen Payne), experiences the murder of his father in his youth.

Further, *Clockers* (1995), based upon the 1992 novel by Richard Price, begins with the compelling melody of Marc Dorsey singing "People in Search of Life", as photos are shown of individuals of color shot and killed by gun violence. The screen offers a montage of those lying in their physical remains, eyes glassy, positioned in manners that active muscle tension rejects. Strike (performed by Mekhi Phifer) is a local community drug dealer who somatically feels the effects of his life choices. Engaged in being "on the streets" and required to perform premeditated kills ordered by his boss, he finds himself with the pains of what appears to be a stomach ulcer. Strike verbalizes explicitly his inability to continue with such behaviors; however, he is groomed and manipulated with false hopes of a wealthy future. And though Strike would seem vulnerable to symptoms of trauma as described by the DSM-V-TR, the supporting characters, homicide detectives that arrive to the scenes of these frequent murders, both Rocco Klein and Larry Mazilli (performed by Harvey Keitel and John Turturro), are the individuals who demonstrate symptomatic behaviors most similar to exposures to trauma as explored below.

In the film *Dead Presidents* (1995), audiences are introduced to characters returning home from the Vietnam War. Though many are proud, they also struggle to reestablish themselves in an economy and community that lacks opportunity. The manner in which Skip (performed by Chris Tucker) emotionally responds to his experiences in the war is explicated and noted as one of a trauma response.

Lastly, within the film *Set It Off* (1996), a supporting character, Francesca (acted by Vivica A. Fox), is shown employed as a bank teller and is asked to relinquish

48   Death and Rebirth to Evolution (1990–1999)

funds to thieves. During the police investigation, she is accused of being connected to the crime and is fired. Her response to this traumatic victimization by both the thieves and betrayal from her employers influences her future decisions, behaviors, and judgment, leaving her to manage trauma symptoms thereafter.

> **Criterion B: Presence of one (or more) of the following intrusion symptoms associated with the traumatic event(s), beginning after the traumatic event(s) occurred: Recurrent, involuntary, and intrusive distressing memories of the traumatic event(s), recurrent distressing dreams in which the content and/or affect of the dream are related to the traumatic event(s), dissociative reactions (e.g., flashbacks) in which the individual feels or acts as if the traumatic event(s) were recurring, intense or prolonged psychological distress at exposure to internal or external cues that symbolize or resemble an aspect of the traumatic event(s), marked physiological reactions to internal or external cues that symbolize or resemble an aspect of the traumatic event(s).**

Jason's Lyric (1994) provides an illustration of intrusive symptomatology that directly parallels criteria of trauma exposure. Jason is a young male who experienced childhood trauma initially by being exposed to chronic domestic violence towards his mother by his physically abusive alcoholic veteran father. Once his father is killed, Jason for years thereafter experiences nightmares pertaining to his father's death and experiences auditory flashbacks that interrupt his ability to establish emotional peace.

Similarly, within the film *Above the Rim* (1994), Shep experiences dreams that wake him in sweats. Shep's nightmares confront him with reliving his best friend's death, significantly impacting his functioning. Nightly, he finds himself playing the same game on basketball courts, touching the backboard, enacting playing basketball and talking with his friend who died. Both of these characters, Jason from *Jason's Lyric* (1994) and Shep from *Above the Rim* (1994), reveal that experiencing distressing nightmares and intrusive thoughts negatively impacts one's lived experience globally.

> **Criterion C: Persistent avoidance of stimuli associated with the traumatic event(s), beginning after the traumatic event(s) occurred, as evidenced by one or both of the following: avoidance of or efforts to avoid distressing memories, thoughts, or feelings about or closely associated with the traumatic event(s), avoidance of or efforts to avoid external reminders (people, places, conversations, activities, objects, situations) that arouse distressing memories, thoughts, or feelings about or closely associated with the traumatic event(s).**

Caine's early chronic childhood exposure to trauma, within *Menace II Society* (1993), structured his perception on the value of life. He noted his father's teachings to cook and sell illegal substances to others significantly influenced the quality of his life, the decisions he made, and his lack of feelings of remorse for his behaviors. When asked directly by his grandfather, an individual who raised him once his mother died of an overdose and father was killed in a drug deal, whether he cared to live or die, Caine indicated that he did not have an answer. Only until he was shot multiple times at the conclusion of the film, losing his own life, was he able to indicate that he in fact did care about living. Caine's choices that maintained his life in perpetual survival mode were an all-encompassing avoidance of examining his traumatic past and the influence it had upon his life. As Caine had numerous traumatic experiences as a child that included witnessing murders, observing his mother's substance use, the death of both of his parents, etc., his ability to process these life events was shelved in service of engaging in a life similar to those of his parents. The cyclical nature of traumas that become intergenerational traumas offers one the ability to avoid confronting and healing from the traumas of the past while creating new traumas in the present.

Poetic Justice (1993) presents Justice as a bereft girlfriend. Contained in most descriptions by her friends and coworkers, Justice is an individual in persistent mourning. Experiencing prolonged grief is understandable after witnessing her boyfriend's death. However, Justice's use of avoidance is a large part of her character as portrayed. Individuals in Justice's life encourage her to engage in life again, pursue dating for example; however, Justice is chronically within the schizoid paranoid position, withdrawn and isolated emotionally. Though Justice utilizes her poetry as a tool to sublimate her feelings, sharing her art with her friend and coworkers, she remains stuck in not being able to reengage with others who are unfamiliar to her. Tentatively trusting only two individuals in her life—her friend who reminds her of her mother who struggled with alcohol use, and her boss—Justice avoids both the conflicts and joys life has to offer.

Within the film *Jason's Lyric* (1994), as noted above, Jason experiences intrusive symptoms of nightmares that compromise his sleep. However, Jason's brother, Joshua (acted by Bookem Woodbine), notes similar symptomatology of intrusive disruptive nightmares as a result of their shared childhood trauma. Josh shares with Jason his excessive use of alcohol quells his dreams, stating, "It's just like garlic, it helps keep the ghosts away". Consequently, rather than work towards healing from his trauma, or be victim to the experience of intrusion from the exposure of the trauma, he avoids his emotions and ideations by drowning himself in substances.

Additionally, Shep within *Above the Rim* (1994) is confronted by his loved ones regarding his changed presentation. Specifically, Shep was a star basketball athlete; yet, once his friend died, he discontinued his athletic pursuits. Though being shepherded into a basketball coaching position at his former high school, he initially rejects the role indicating that he no longer identified with the game, avoiding the sport and his talent due to his feelings of guilt for his friend's death. Further, Shep was confronted by loved ones that when he became emotionally triggered he tended to abandon the situation and consequently the person. His response outlined

50 Death and Rebirth to Evolution (1990–1999)

his lack of feeling connected and attached, while self-acknowledging his tendency to leave emotionally difficult situations. Consequently, he later described himself as a "runner". As life continued in his former neighborhood, at his former high school, Shep struggled to reconnect, form relationships, and heal from the guilt, shame, and responsibility that he felt due to the death of his friend.

Further, Detectives Klein and Mazilli in *Clockers* (1995) exhibit a superb illustration of avoidance and how such a symptom can arise due to chronic exposures to trauma within one's employment. When dispatched to investigate a homicide, Detectives Klein and Mazilli within the vehicle prepare themselves to examine a body that has been victimized by gun violence. They retrieve two shots of alcohol and quickly consume them while driving to the scene. Upon arrival, they begin, with colleagues, to examine the body making comments as to the number of shots, entry and exit wounds, and other observations typical of an individual in their role. However, these detectives approach the experience as a comedy act, making jokes, laughing, and engaging in a banter that appears inhumane given the purpose they are there to serve. When the body is identified, Detective Mazilli makes comment that he is familiar with the victim, having known the victim since his childhood. As this might render one to reflect upon the gravity of the situation, he continues with Detective Klein, responding in a similar manner when Detective Klein offers an additional diverting comment that makes light of the lost life in front of them. Both Detectives Klein and Mazilli's use of alcohol to numb the experience of their work coupled with what could be interpreted as the use of a higher-order defense, humor, are used to avoid the emotional impact these traumatic duties have upon their psyche.

Criterion D: Negative alterations in cognitions and mood associated with the traumatic event(s), beginning or worsening after the traumatic event(s) occurred, as evidenced by two (or more) of the following: inability to remember an important aspect of the traumatic event(s), persistent and exaggerated negative beliefs or expectations about oneself, others, or the world, persistent, distorted cognitions about the cause or consequences of the traumatic event(s) that lead the individual to blame himself/herself or others, persistent negative emotional state (e.g., fear, horror, anger, guilt, or shame), markedly diminished interest or participation in significant activities, feelings of detachment or estrangement from others, persistent inability to experience positive emotions (e.g., inability to experience happiness, satisfaction, or loving feelings).

This criterion for this specific diagnosis was most commonly offered within characters, and in many cases was a significant aspect of the themes which the films' scripts rested upon. Doughboy, acted by Ice Cube in the film *Boyz N The*

Hood (1991), is introduced as a young man recently released from prison. Though connected with his friends and family, he is not afraid to protect his loved ones in life-threatening situations, and appears detached from others' experience of pain he inflicted upon them. Doughboy feels abandoned by his mother who lacks outward loving affection towards him. He equally feels abandoned by the system that remains absent and silent, not advocating for the betterment of his community and circumstance. The chronicity of violence and traumatic events aforementioned in the film that causes Doughboy as a child to see a dead body on the streets with his friends and to state the infamous statement, "Either they don't know…don't show…or don't care about what's going on in the hood" imprints upon this character and fosters his limited value for his own life and others'.

Additionally, Justice within *Poetic Justice* (1993) finds herself in such grief that she is detached and struggles to be able to engage in behaviors typical for her age. Though she is encouraged to find herself and what she enjoys in life, she is uninterested and repelled at the thought of doing so. Her ability to experience positive affect is blunted, where she seems to have forgotten how to smile and find delight in life's experiences. Despite individuals offering support, Justice minimizes the importance happiness and positive emotional experiences hold in her life.

Above the Rim (1994) portrays Shep as an individual who distorts the reality regarding the fate of his best friend. He blames himself for his death and engages in the world in a manner that reflects that he is cloaked within the death instinct. Shep walks slowly, is disengaged, isolated, and lacks typical responses within situations that evoke engagement from others. His persistent sadness and grief cause him to terminate playing basketball perhaps prematurely. Despite the events that occur around him that warrant a chuckle, Shep finds himself unable to engage in positive affect or offer a behavioral matching to the situation by appearing humored. As a result, Shep presents as withdrawn, unable to relate to others, and emotionally cold.

Further, *Set It Off* (1996) depicts this criterion with perfect accuracy. Francesca, once a victim of an armed robbery at her place of employment and fired thereafter for an inability to perform protocol during the event, experiences trauma responses. Her presentation includes an exaggerated negative belief and expectations about others and the world while displaying a persistent anger about how the world treats people like her. When her friends attempt to convince her otherwise about her beliefs, she buckles down and is unwilling to view herself as anything other than a victim that is justified in becoming the aggressor due to the unfairness of the world. Such a belief propels her to successfully adopt an identification with the aggressor to regain a sense of control over her life. Rather than feel like the victim of an armed robbery and a victim of corporations that do not believe in her, she becomes an advocate for robbing banks with her friends. Consequently, she begins to enact behaviors that both victimize and potentially traumatize others. The stark difference in Francesca's behaviors from before the robbery in which she was a victim, to after the robbery, is striking in understanding the influence trauma can have on shifting one's emotional presentation.

> **Criterion E:** Marked alterations in arousal and reactivity associated with the traumatic event(s), beginning or worsening after the traumatic event(s) occurred, as evidenced by two (or more) of the following: irritable behavior and angry outbursts (with little or no provocation), typically expressed as verbal or physical aggression toward people or objects, reckless or self-destructive behavior, hypervigilance, exaggerated startle response, problems with concentration, sleep disturbance.

Three films in particular highlight the above criterion within their characters. For instance, within the film *Juice* (1992), Q (performed by Omar Epps) begins the film with a group of three friends that were referred to as "their crew". These friends cared for and took care of one another; however, once a member of his crew killed a store clerk, he found his friend's ability to modulate his murderous rage was extinguished. As a reaction to killing the clerk, Bishop (performed by Tupac Shakur) came to accept his lack of respect of individuals' humanity, even those closest to him. As a result, when his friends confront him regarding his choice to kill the store clerk and verbalize upset regarding his behavior, Bishop acts out by shooting one and beginning to hunt the remainder of them. In response, Q attempts to find ways to keep himself safe from Bishop while acknowledging that there were limited outcomes: most likely, options that were dire and would result in the death of Bishop or himself. Once Q obtained a firearm for protection, when a homeless man in an alley makes a noise, Q draws his gun and looks the man in his eyes as he pleads with Q not to kill him. At that time, Q questions what is happening to him and makes the decision to rid himself of the gun. What has happened to him includes being exposed to a trauma caused by Bishop, a teen with a history of violence, and fearing that he has limited time remaining being alive as Bishop will follow through on his threats to his life.

Within *Menace II Society* (1993), the audience is provided a childhood history of the lead character, Caine. It is shared that though he engages in numerous illegal behaviors, he has never taken the life of another individual. It is not until he is shot and witnesses his cousin, the only person in life he felt safe with, being killed through a violent traumatic act, that Caine reacts by possessing the desire to gain revenge on the individuals who shot his cousin. Caine learns that after killing a man, he responds by being numb, lacking emotion tied to his behavior; and he acknowledges to himself that, if needed, he could repeat a similar murderous act in the future.

Upon reflection, Shep, the lead of *Above the Rim* (1994), is observed experiencing hypervigilant behaviors that add to his traumatic presentation. At the onset of the film, Shep is easily startled by an individual who places their hand on his shoulder to gain his attention when asking whether his seat at a table was vacant. Though he does not appear to be finished, once startled, he gets up and leaves without further interaction.

Further, the film *Jason's Lyric* (1994) does not provide information regarding the brothers', Jason's and Joshua's, history prior to the night of their father's death. However, Joshua is presented as being a "problem child" even into his adulthood. His mother Gloria (performed by Suzzanne Douglas) holds a negative esteem for him based upon the numerous ways in which he disappoints her. Within the family dynamic, Jason who engages with his mother and respects her is held as the "good son", creating a visible split, allowing the negative within the family to be disavowed and projected onto Joshua. When Joshua is released from prison within the first scenes, the audience is able to glean support that his behaviors are characterized by recklessness and are self-destructive. At the conclusion of the film, Joshua's recklessness and self-destructive behaviors become a literal visual expression that results in the demise of himself and others.

With the quantity of films that address traumatic events based in daily violence, this decade of film production could leave audiences screening these films wondering: Are these experiences the life of African Americans in America? Are African Americans' energies consumed by drug, crime, murder, death, and consistent sprints fleeing from authorities? Are African Americans' existence riddled with stagnation that is influenced by countless individual and systemic issues creating shadows of sadness, sorrow, fear, and hopelessness on an entire community of individuals? And, as one attempts to peel away the vicarious traumatic layer that is left behind once screening these stories, these narratives shine a light that the thunder heard in specific communities where people of color tend to reside creates agitation and increased levels of violence. Only the few find solace and a peaceful quiet as suggested in *Jason's Lyric* (1994). And though these films highlighted the range of symptoms that are characteristic of PTSD, we find that some when exposed to traumas exhibit a numbness where their humanity deactivates, their empathy for others' humanity is minimized, and, in the worst cases, disappears. Under these circumstances, we find that these individuals present with social maladjustment, which manifests in symptoms that typically are characterized by (but perhaps do not accurately represent) diagnoses and traits of conduct disorder (*Juice*, 1992; *Menace II Society*, 1993) for those who are minors and diagnosed as antisocial personality disorder for those who are adults (*Menace II Society*, 1993; *Jason's Lyric*, 1994; and *Set It Off*, 1996).

Similarly to yesteryear and the years to follow, the psychological influence these films have continues to perpetuate previous negative stereotypes of individuals of color. Viewing year after year that one's life is vulnerable to being disposable by violence and internalizing the messages of characters who express "I ain't shit, and you ain't shit" (*Juice*, 1992) while questioning whether life is worth living and acknowledging that one's lived choices are "suicidal" (*Menace II Society*, 1993) offer audiences an opportunity to walk in the hopelessness that individuals of all colors may feel in communities saturated in violence. Internalized stereotypes of gangsters, criminals, and accurately portrayed symptoms of diagnoses that ignore the exquisite sides of humanity impact the psyche of those who view. Historically, within the United States we understand that there have been numerous attempts to poison the internal understanding of whom persons of color can be in America. Creating films to offer audiences a manner to reflect and represent who they are is a delicate responsibility. Developing and greenlighting films that portray persons of color in these ways provide a platform for individuals to identify with the characters and see themselves within the characters, holding "I AM" this character, I can be this character, and I am afraid of being victimized by this character. For those who lacked the emotional tolerance for these films, holding that I cannot identify with this character and I will not be this character can create fear regarding what the future in reality holds for one of color. These films collectively grossed over one billion dollars in the American markets alone (Box Office Mojo, 2024), which suggests that they were successful blockbusters that influenced generations of audiences, further inculcating the familiar stereotypes of African Americans while telling the stories of many Black people in America.

Conversely, audiences are also offered a view of individuals who demonstrate resilience and protective factors that suggest that a life of violence is a temporary experience. When an environment of safety is desired and worked towards actualization (*Boyz N The Hood*, 1991; *Menace II Society*, 1993; *Above the Rim*, 1994; *Jason's Lyric*, 1994), we observe that the characters' agitation is lessened. Though many of the films conclude with a feel-good ending, no conclusion can erase the horror, the trauma, sadness, hopelessness, helplessness, and grief these stories share.

Family

According to the Oxford Dictionary, a family is "a group of one or more parents and their children living together as a unit; all the descendants of a common ancestor; and designed to be suitable for children as well as adults" (Oxford Languages, 2023). Within the decade of the 1990s the notion of family was shown literally within films and the concept of family was challenged to be widened from its original definition. Films such as *The Best Man* (1991), *The Five Heartbeats* (1991), *Waiting to Exhale* (1995), *The Preacher's Wife* (1996), *Soul Food* (1997), *Life* (1999), and *The Wood* (1999) depicted relationships that suggest that despite lacking blood relations, intimacies within friendship coupled with engaging in life's milestones and shifts in emotional maturation together can create dynamics that resemble family dynamics closely.

A musical, *The Five Heartbeats* (1991) depicts a narrative of five young men attempting to make their talents known by performing original music in the 1970s. This film, based upon various musical groups of the time, shares the story of The Five Heartbeats' trajectory from a new vocal group to a place of fame. Four members of The Five Heartbeats' family experiences are shared with little elaboration, yet we are able to glean from the short scenes the various influences family bonds can have upon individuals and the course of their life decisions. For example, Duck (performed by Robert Townsend) and J.T. (acted by Leon) are biological brothers. Their large family lives in humble housing, sharing beds together, and maintaining an emotional strong connection amongst them. Eddie, the lead singer (performed by Michael Wright), is seen to have a father, Eddie, Sr., that shares with him, "You ain't gon be shit, cuz I ain't shit". Eddie, Sr. understands his warning to his son to be one of love rather than of fear, self-hate, and discouragement. Further, Choirboy (performed by Tico Wells) is met with his father who is adamant regarding his lack of approval of him participating in singing secular music growing up as a preacher's son. Despite achieving early success performing on the Chitlin' Circuit, he continues to experience conflicts with his father regarding his decision to tour. Though varying familial relations are illustrated, once these young men became adults, their experiences reflected their early childhood parental influences. For example, Duck and J.T. once experiencing financial success are seen purchasing a large family home that accommodates their large family of origin. The family is well-dressed and made ecstatic by the surprise of this gift. Eddie, Jr. falls into significant substance abuse taking time to learn how to care for, love, and value himself in the absence of demonstrative love from his father. Choirboy concludes finding his way to his father's desire of being active within the church. *The Five Heartbeats* shows that early childhood experiences with parents are significant in the journey one has to becoming an adult, while illustrating that a brotherhood between young men becoming adults is equally important for a feeling of unconditional support and finding self-love.

In 1995 *Waiting to Exhale*, a film of four middle-aged women, grew mass appeal across generations. Dissimilar to the nostalgic coming-of-age stories, four women are introduced coming into their own when challenging life transitions are navigated. The four female friends present with appealing lifestyles. They have close, loving friendships, careers, and family bonds. However, their deeper emotional experience and challenges held within their dating, love, and marital experiences lead the audience to experience great sadness and sorrow for these characters, while celebrating in their triumphs and joy equally. What is imprinted is the importance of possessing support from loved ones, a sisterhood, which facilitates emotional growth that can happen at any age. Despite differences amongst the women, people can find sisterhood in the similarities and support the differences each one brings with a lack of judgment and with love.

The Preacher's Wife (1996) depicts the humble home of Reverend Henry Biggs (performed by Courtney B. Vance), his wife Julia (acted by Whitney Houston), Jeremiah (introducing Justin Pierre Edmund), and his mother-in-law, Margueritte (performed by Jenifer Lewis). Reverend Biggs presents as a man burdened by the demands of his aging church. He shepherds and serves a lower-income neighborhood attempting to meet the needs of his community. Equally, he presents as no longer a cheerful servant, rather his affect is apathetic. He fears his contribution to the community does not influence change for the lives of those around him, including his family. Reverend Biggs' doubt in himself causes him to show up for others as a shell of his past self. Though he demonstrates a willingness to follow through on his obligation, he is unable to muster further passion to invest more of himself into his work, his role as a father, and as a husband. When he asks for help from God, he is unable to be readily accepting of the acts of his angel, Dudley (performed by Denzel Washington). Within this holiday feel-good film about a mentally, physically, and spiritually fatigued preacher we are able to witness one who begins to light his candle again creating a flame that sparks and energizes not only him, but also his community. This rejuvenation allows Reverend Biggs to remember his values and whom he can be when he arrives mindfully to the spaces he occupies. At the onset of the film his symptoms of burnout from acute stressors in the midst of various transitions demonstrate how debilitating a diagnosis of Adjustment Disorder with Mixed Emotions can be for an individual. The audience is also able to view how protective factors such as family, community, and prayer can elevate one to be their best self.

Soul Food (1997), starring Vanessa Williams, Nia Long, Vivica A. Fox, and Brandon Hammond, depicts a close-knit family representing three generations of love. With a value on remaining connected by having weekly Sunday dinners with all members of the family present, audiences are able to see the strength of a family unit. Within this construct, individuals most close and cared for are supported; and, when needed, forgiveness is generously offered for those who have caused hurt and have betrayed. *Soul Food* acknowledges the imperfections, meaning the conflicts family systems hold. Such conflicts included aggressive reactions, infidelity, competition between siblings, and challenges that are felt when one desires support from the unit but does not receive what they require at the time. Despite these relationship challenges, there remains a commonality that acts as a glue that keeps the family system connected even when presented with what appears to be a difficult feat.

The Wood (1999) presents a coming-of-age story following the academic and social path of four adolescent boys from middle school until the first of the group is married. *The Wood* shows the longitudinal trajectory of what brotherhood can be. With each of the groomsmen's families gathered in celebration of the union of one of the members of the friend group, the biological family units of these young men extend beyond themselves and have formed a multigenerational community. Though not related by bloodlines, these boys over time grow into brothers. They offer one another a similar meaningful support to that which can be provided by one's biological family of origin.

Further, *The Best Man* (1991), directed by Malcolm D. Lee, similarly follows the friendship of four men who became familiar with one another in college during times of life transitions. Beginning to support one another through commitments of career, love, and marriage, the four are challenged to not only fulfill their personal desires but consider what is best for their friends. As these men note that they perceive their relationship as a brotherhood, similarly to *The Wood* (1999), we find that despite the conflicts they experience, their bond based upon honesty yields a relationship that is everlasting. In particular, *The Best Man* (1991) was so well received that their brotherhood continued to be depicted within the feature *The Best Man Holiday* in 2013 and again on the Peacock series, *The Best Man: The Final Chapter* (2022).

Familial bonds that we are born into at times provide an individual with love, acceptance, and support that are required to live a fulfilling life. For others, life that is full of transitions, shifts, and evolution also requires the love of a family that is self-made by people who know your core and provide you with a particular desired way of being nurtured. As these films follow the lives of various characters, the commonality amongst them suggests that despite time and circumstances, bonds that include a brotherhood, a sisterhood, and family, regardless of how they are constructed, can last a lifetime. As the definition of family is noted to include "all the descendants of a common ancestor" one may suggest that individuals who belong to the African/Black diaspora are just that, all family.

Loving Passionately

When one experiences a death, desire to embrace living can be a powerful urge. Individuals can experience death and grief in many ways, though one loss that cannot be ignored is when someone loses a love accompanied by regret. There may remain possibilities of generating "What ifs" about lingering actions of the past and "What ifs" for future actions that are likely difficult to actualize. While sitting in the limbo of vexation, time beats on and one experiences anticlimactic moments devoid of gratification and love. However, when one reconciles with themselves that the love once had is no longer readily available, there remains an opportunity to position oneself in a vigorous act of humility, crafting a desperate plea to declare love. The films *Mo' Better Blues* (1990), *Boomerang* (1992), *Love Jones* (1997), and *How Stella Got Her Groove Back* (1998) present similar themes amongst four diverse characters within these films.

Mo' Better Blues (1990)

Bleek (acted by Denzel Washington) is an established trumpeter leading a band that performs in a popular jazz club in New York. Within this environment, Bleek maintains a business and friend relationship with his bandmates and his long-time committed friend and manager, Giant (performed by Spike Lee). Bleek also has love interests with two women, Indigo (portrayed by Joie Lee), a small-statured school teacher with natural hair and brown skin, and Clarke (played by Cynda Williams), a tall singer with caramel skin and naturally straight hair. These two women, who present in varying ways from one another, are aware of Bleek's engagements with one another and desire him to make a choice regarding with whom he would like to become romantically exclusive. Despite their requests for him to figure out "what you want", Bleek continues to attempt to manage both relationships creating a complicated love triangle.

When Bleek is unable to determine whom he would like to continue to pursue and which relationship he would like to terminate, both women decide to discontinue the relationship they have with him. Bleek is alone and most concerned regarding Giant's gambling debt that results in individuals hunting Giant to physically injure

58 Death and Rebirth to Evolution (1990–1999)

him to encourage payments. However, on a night Bleek fires his saxophonist and must solo with his remaining bandmates, he is unable to leave the stage swiftly and rescue Giant from being severely physically assaulted when confronted about his debt. When Bleek arrives, he finds his friend unconscious lying in trash in the rear of the club, and facing his friend's assailants. In upset, Bleek swings to hit one of the men which incites the assailants to attack him in a similar fashion. At the conclusion of the fight, one uses Bleek's trumpet to strike his mouth, leaving him unconscious and his lips permanently marred, unable to play the trumpet as he once had. Bleek is found hospitalized; and when released, he is depressed and bleak regarding the promise of his future.

As Bleek is physically healing, he presents as a man who is emotionally crumbling. He is isolated; and we learn that he refuses visits from others which results in people not seeing him for months. Indigo indicates that, because of his depression, she did not know whether he was alive or dead. He holds conversations with himself and the music he listens to, begins to neglect his grooming, and his living environment is in disarray. Upon one uneventful evening, Bleek arrives to a jazz club to accept an invitation to accompany his former saxophonist, Shadow (fulfilled by Wesley Snipes), and reenters the world of his past. He presents as a shadow of his former self, no longer to be the adroit trumpeter of his yesterday, rather now, identity-less. It appears that Bleek did not account for the fact that "human identity is a complex process" that is "constantly evolving" (Marquez, 2014, p. 143). Rather, disappointed in himself, he leaves the stage midway through the song, exits the club, and hands his trumpet to Giant in an act of retirement. Bleek begins to walk, stops, and soaked from the rain finds himself on Indigo's apartment stoop.

Though Indigo was deceived, betrayed, and abandoned by Bleek, in his desperation he asks her to recall, hold, and embrace the love that she once had for him. Indigo is consciously aware of Bleek's request as illustrated by her response to him, "You want me to save your life", and Bleek is equally as clear: "Yes, save my life", he begs. In his efforts to locate his identity, Bleek's plea is ultimately a request to be seen, to be told and shown that he is worthy. He begs "to be recognized, dignified and esteemed" (Marquez, 2014, p. 148) by her. In the short moments she has with Bleek, she wrestles with her logical self and emotional self. Her logical self is emotionally defended as demonstrated by her physically turning away from him. She displays her anger and hurt by reenacting what she experienced from him: rejection. However, Indigo relents to her emotional self, appeasing her desire to be loved by the man she loves, and saves his life.

Boomerang (1992)

Freud's personality theory (1923) suggested that the human psyche was constructed upon structures that included the tripartite id, ego, and superego. Though these areas of personality are created and refined at various developmental stages in a person's life, they are understood to be a part of one's personality construct. The id is a result of the unconscious mind, manifested by engaging in one's impulses, early childhood desires, and having a desire to feel good or enact the Pleasure Principle as Freud coined. The id's biological make-up includes the Libidinal Drive (sex, life, nurturing, etc.) and the Death Instinct (Thanatos: characterized as aggression, violence, and sabotage). The ego that lives between the conscious and unconscious mind teeters between the id and the superego, working with reason to indulge the id, yet with limitations presented from the real world that has consequences and re-sponsibilities. Further, the superego engages as one's conscience and reflects moral values of external influences such as ideals adopted from one's parents, family, and society. The superego determines what one "should do", what is "right" and "wrong", or otherwise allows one to manage the id's urges that are sexual and ag-gressive in nature.

Marcus (performed by Eddie Murphy) is a successful advertising executive hopeful of attaining the newly vacant director position within the company he is employed by. Upon a business merger, Marcus soon learns that his desired director position has recently been occupied by Jacqueline (acted by Robyn Givens). This attractive, successful, creative man is a womanizer, a walking id of his sexual im-pulses who dates many women briefly in an effort to locate the "perfect" woman. Marcus' search is performed in a superficial manner, as made evident by his deter-mining whether one is compatible based upon possessing a manicured pedicure, as he looks for a woman to match him in success and esteem. Marcus' friend, Gerard (acted by David Alan Grier), offers Marcus frequently a superego perspective that is often heard and respected, yet disregarded by Marcus when he continues to make similar choices regarding whom he will pursue.

However, once dating Jacqueline, Marcus declares he believes he loves her. She is poised, accomplished, and unmistakably a boss. She presents as a mirror to Mar-cus, as their values are synced. Yet, their relationship is presented to be the result of Freudian id impulses that connect them, rather than a reflection of a substantial personal connection. When challenges arise within the relationship that cause Mar-cus to terminate his relationship with Jacqueline, he finds a surprising connection to his and Jacqueline's coworker, Angela (conveyed by Halle Berry). During his committed relationship with Angela, Marcus engages in a sexual encounter with Jacqueline that damages the trust he had with Angela. Once Angela learns of this, she terminates the relationship, and leaves hurt and betrayed.

Despite continuing to engage with Jacqueline once his relationship with Angela concludes, Marcus understands that his connection to Jacqueline is less fulfilling and meaningful in comparison to the relationship he cultivated with Angela. There-after, Marcus demonstrates efforts to gain the attention of Angela once more, to no avail. Dejected, Marcus engages Angela's former art students from a community center to arrive to her new place of employment, forcing an opportunity to speak with her. After confronting her with his previous unanswered gestures, he notes missing her. When asked to offer one reason why she should "take you back", Mar-cus' silence was palpable, generating only the question of whether she still loved him. Marcus declares his love for her by stating, "I'm miserable. I can't breathe without you. I can't breathe" and they succumb to an embracing kiss. It is then that

Marcus graduates from working primarily from his id in romantic relationships to fully inviting the consciousness of his ego, to gain a greater integration of a true connection with another.

Higher Learning (1995)

Within emerging adulthood, individuals have the opportunity to learn about themselves while being exposed to a myriad of peers with varying identities. This time allows one to explore, be curious, and wonder regarding what is possible in life. Upon college campuses, a diverse set of individuals are asked to come together, create a community, and enact the culture of the academic institution. However, conflicts can ensue and differences amongst groups can become intolerable creating ruptures, destruction, and pain leading to feelings of grief amidst learning a great deal about others and oneself.

Higher Learning (1995) portrays the characters of Malik (performed by Omar Epps), Kristen (acted by Kristy Swanson), and Remy (performed by Michael Rapaport). All from differing backgrounds, they find themselves at the onset of university having the same experience, locating themselves in the space and searching for interpersonal connection while being receptive to the academic and life education being provided. Within this time, Kristen explores healing from a sexual assault that occurs during a party early in her matriculation and begins to explore her sexuality. As Malik examines what it means to obtain an education upon an athletic scholarship and struggles to perform what is required of him to be a successful academic student, he also attempts to understand what it means to be an African American male in the United States attending a primarily White institution. And Remy, a White male, has difficulty finding where he fits with his same-aged peers. He finds solace when he is accepted by a Neo-Nazi group, and is led down a road of psychological grooming. He is massaged to sculpt his disappointments into honed hate for other cultures in an effort to blame all others for his challenges.

When viewing Remy, what is witnessed is an evocation of what Freud coined as the uncanny offering audiences the ability to watch the very essence of this character slowly escape him to become replaced by vitriol and a vessel of violence. Growing concern for Remy happens early within the film, slowly feeling the hope of his character wither as the pressure of college increases and his lack of ability to navigate these demands rises. With dismay and the invitation to place his negative feelings into a subject, Remy becomes an ideal candidate to enact hate: in this case, racial hate. The uncanny settles amongst the viewers when the music lifts and Remy exposes his shaven head. In this moment, all of Remy's previously contained "bad", what we observe as sadness and loneliness, is exposed and "...everything that was intended to remain secret, hidden away, has come into the open" (Freud et al., 2003, p. 132). Freud continues that "the **uncanny** (*das unheimlich-liche, 'the unhomely'*) is in some way a species of the **familiar** (*das heimliche, 'the homely'*)" (Freud et al., 2003, p. 134). Indeed, Remy looks familiar, but he who entered college is gone, suppressed deeply at best, leaving all to know that this is the eye of the perfect storm and thunderous sounds of murderous rage ominously await before us.

Though there are grief and sadness for the bereft, these characters showed that individuals can find solidarity and a sense of belonging and community in the face of traumatic events. Loving one another, love for one's shared identity group and community, and loving one's beliefs are all passionately offered in this film. *Higher Learning* (1995) supports that though there are circumstances that derail, humanity can be empathized with across color, ethnicity, and differing identity creeds bringing people together rather than wedging individuals apart.

Love Jones (1997)

Love triangles are a common presence within films of romance. Love entanglements create a tension within the characters and how they relate allowing intrigue in the plot to blossom. Love triangles additionally introduce an Oedipal dynamic, three individuals with an element of competition and envy within the relationship. *Love Jones*, a film starring Larenz Tate as Darius and Nia Long as Nina, depicts a romantic relationship filled with possibility and love. Yet, conflicts arise in their relationship due to the presence of triangles that exist that interlope in the love that Darius and Nina have for one another.

At the onset of Nina and Darius' intimate relationship, Nina shares her concern that the timing is not the best for her to pursue a relationship. However, due to the significantly compelling attraction had between the two, she falls into a relationship with him despite her reservations. Indeed, Nina was accurate in her assessment of the timing of the relationship. The couple experiences their first challenge as a result of Nina introducing a third party to their couple. Marvin, her ex-boyfriend who resides in New York, is visited to "take care of unfinished business" according to Nina. As a result, she travels to the city and attempts to understand her position and feelings for Marvin. When a third enters the relationship, it creates a competition for Darius where he defensively responds with indifference and deceives Nina into believing he is apathetic to her decision to explore the quality of her previous relationship. Ultimately, his response minimizes the emotional connection he has for her, leaving her hurt and willing to walk away from the relationship she has with him to resolve her former relationship with Marvin. Yet, from an alternative angle, Darius' defensive response also protected all involved from creating a love triangle. Specifically, if he could place himself outside of the committed relationship with Nina, this would allow her the space to learn her desires in his absence. However, Darius' defenses used to protect him from disappointment, pain, and hurt proved futile. Despite his attempt to mask his feelings from Nina and equally from himself, he is reluctantly aware of his sadness and grief. He also contends that no defense mechanism, including suppression and humor, can reduce the gravity felt by Nina's absence.

Once Nina returns to Chicago, after terminating her previous relationship, she desires to connect with Darius. On a day in the city, Nina sees Darius with a woman, an individual Nina understands to be a love interest. Consequently, she does not reach out to him, and rather sees him with friends a different evening. When Darius confronts her regarding her return to Chicago and not reaching out to him, she indicates that she was providing him space due to his relationship with the woman she saw him with. Scenes thereafter, we see that Nina and Darius are able to rekindle their relationship, yet Nina questions Darius' commitment to her, holding the fantasy that there is a third within their relationship, his previous girlfriend. Though Darius shares with Nina a number of times that he has no further connection to his ex-girlfriend, the imagined other in the relationship simmers mistrust and discord that result in hostile exchanges with one another and finally the demise of their relationship.

Love Jones is unique in the manner in which both characters, Nina and Darius, are shown to have the opportunity for a love interest outside of the relationship they hold with one another. When their relationship experiences conflict, it does so twice for the same reason: a third is introduced to the relationship and their alliance to one another does not withstand the conflict. As both parties fall victim to the feeling of competition in the relationship, neither character is manipulated or taken advantage of more than the other. Nina is no more victimized in the relationship than Darius because they both experienced bringing a third, actualized and imagined, into the relationship. This equality illustrated within the characters allows *Love Jones* to have a greater appeal to a wide audience as a result.

Though, *Love Jones* concludes in a conventional fashion, with a love proclamation from Darius to Nina. After she publicly shares her experience of loving Darius in a poem, meeting him in his language as a writer and poet, he finds her outside, in the rain. Despite Nina mentioning the timing remains not optimum, as she has relocated to reside in New York, distance and circumstance are of no consequence and will not hinder regaining the love that was once paused.

How Stella Got Her Groove Back (1998)

The busyness and business of life can distort the perception of time. When one chronically has a great deal on their plate, one may either falsely feel time has stopped or wait for other aspects of life to happen. Enjoyment, holidays, and spending time with loved ones can be shelved to manage one's daily demands. However, in the face of loss, one can awaken the courage to embrace life's pleasures. Within the film *How Stella Got Her Groove Back*, we are introduced to a forty-year-old cisgender woman who finds herself committed to the life she has created which significantly shifts when numerous life events occur.

Stella (acted by Angela Bassett) is what most would consider to be a successful woman. She is gainfully employed in the money markets, is well-esteemed in her career, has a son whom she primarily raises after her divorce, and has lifelong loved ones that she connects with interpersonally. Yet, her manicured life at work and the home she sustains are saturated in loss, where her ten-year-old son reminds her that she struggles to positively engage in fun. Though Stella attempts to convince him she is able to have fun, he provides her the most serious look a youngster can muster and reiterates his desire for her. It appears that, at this time, Stella is first reminded that she has lost a part of her ability to enjoy life.

Once at home and spending alone time reminiscing with a glass of wine and family photos, Stella experiences a projection of herself (that manifests within the childhood desires, and having a desire to feel good or enact the Pleasure Principle as Freud coined. The id's biological make-up includes the Libidinal Drive (sex, life, nurturing, etc.) and the Death Instinct (Thanatos: characterized as aggression, violence, and sabotage). The ego that lives between the conscious and unconscious mind teeters between the id and the superego, working with reason to indulge the id, yet with limitations presented from the real world that has consequences and responsibilities. Further, the superego engages as one's conscience and reflects moral values of external influences such as ideals adopted from one's parents, family, and society. The superego determines what one "should do", what is "right" and "wrong", or otherwise allows one to manage the id's urges that are sexual and aggressive in nature.

Marcus (performed by Eddie Murphy) is a successful advertising executive hopeful of attaining the newly vacant director position within the company he is employed by. Upon a business merger, Marcus soon learns that his desired director position has recently been occupied by Jacqueline (acted by Robyn Givens). This attractive, successful, creative man is a womanizer, a walking id of his sexual impulses who dates many women briefly in an effort to locate the "perfect" woman. Marcus' search is performed in a superficial manner, as made evident by his determining whether one is compatible based upon possessing a manicured pedicure, as he looks for a woman to match him in success and esteem. Marcus' friend, Gerard (acted by David Alan Grier), offers Marcus frequently a superego perspective that is often heard and respected, yet disregarded by Marcus when he continues to make similar choices regarding whom he will pursue.

However, once dating Jacqueline, Marcus declares he believes he loves her. She is poised, accomplished, and unmistakably a boss. She presents as a mirror to Marcus, as their values are synced. Yet, their relationship is presented to be the result of Freudian id impulses that connect them, rather than a reflection of a substantial personal connection. When challenges arise within the relationship that cause Marcus to terminate his relationship with Jacqueline, he finds a surprising connection to his and Jacqueline's coworker, Angela (conveyed by Halle Berry). During his committed relationship with Angela, Marcus engages in a sexual encounter with Jacqueline that damages the trust he had with Angela. Once Angela learns of this, she terminates the relationship, and leaves hurt and betrayed.

Despite continuing to engage with Jacqueline once his relationship with Angela concludes, Marcus understands that his connection to Jacqueline is less fulfilling and meaningful in comparison to the relationship he cultivated with Angela. Thereafter, Marcus demonstrates efforts to gain the attention of Angela once more, to no avail. Dejected, Marcus engages Angela's former art students from a community center to arrive to her new place of employment, forcing an opportunity to speak with her. After confronting her with his previous unanswered gestures, he notes missing her. When asked to offer one reason why she should "take you back", Marcus' silence was palpable, generating only the question of whether she still loved him. Marcus declares his love for her by stating, "I'm miserable. I can't breathe without you. I can't breathe" and they succumb to an embracing kiss. It is then that

60 Death and Rebirth to Evolution (1990–1999)

Marcus graduates from working primarily from his id in romantic relationships to fully inviting the consciousness of his ego, to gain a greater integration of a true connection with another.

Higher Learning (1995)

Within emerging adulthood, individuals have the opportunity to learn about themselves while being exposed to a myriad of peers with varying identities. This time allows one to explore, be curious, and wonder regarding what is possible in life. Upon college campuses, a diverse set of individuals are asked to come together, create a community, and enact the culture of the academic institution. However, conflicts can ensue and differences amongst groups can become intolerable creating ruptures, destruction, and pain leading to feelings of grief amidst learning a great deal about others and oneself.

Higher Learning (1995) portrays the characters of Malik (performed by Omar Epps), Kristen (acted by Kristy Swanson), and Remy (performed by Michael Rapaport). All from differing backgrounds, they find themselves at the onset of university having the same experience, locating themselves in the space and searching for interpersonal connection while being receptive to the academic and life education being provided. Within this time, Kristen explores healing from a sexual assault that occurs during a party early in her matriculation and begins to explore her sexuality. As Malik examines what it means to obtain an education upon an athletic scholarship and struggles to perform what is required of him to be a successful academic student, he also attempts to understand what it means to be an African American male in the United States attending a primarily White institution. And Remy, a White male, has difficulty finding where he fits with his same-aged peers. He finds solace when he is accepted by a Neo-Nazi group, and is led down a road of psychological grooming. He is massaged to sculpt his disappointments into honed hate for other cultures in an effort to blame all others for his challenges.

When viewing Remy, what is witnessed is an evocation of what Freud coined as the uncanny offering audiences the ability to watch the very essence of this character slowly escape him to become replaced by vitriol and a vessel of violence. Growing concern for Remy happens early within the film, slowly feeling the hope of his character wither as the pressure of college increases and his lack of ability to navigate these demands rises. With dismay and the invitation to place his negative feelings into a subject, Remy becomes an ideal candidate to enact hate: in this case, racial hate. The uncanny settles amongst the viewers when the music lifts and Remy exposes his shaven head. In this moment, all of Remy's previously contained "bad", what we observe as sadness and loneliness, is exposed and "…everything that was intended to remain secret, hidden away, has come into the open" (Freud et al., 2003, p. 132). Freud continues that "the **uncanny** (*das unheimlich-liche, 'the unhomely'*) is in some way a species of the **familiar** (*das heimliche, 'the homely'*)" (Freud et al., 2003, p. 134). Indeed, Remy looks familiar, but he who entered college is gone, suppressed deeply at best, leaving all to know that this is the eye of the perfect storm and thunderous sounds of murderous rage ominously await before us.

film as a visual hallucination coupled with ideas of reference) in Jamaica on holiday. Seizing the moment, she invites her friend, Delilah (performed by Whoopi Goldberg), to join her on the island. Moments after she does so, she asks that her friend ignores the invitation she extended due to the reality of her life's demands. With Delilah's encouragement, Stella follows through with her suggestion and begins a vacation in Jamaica.

Once in Jamaica, Stella is introduced to Winston (performed by Taye Diggs) over breakfast at the hotel. Finding herself awakened by him, she sees herself interested, and aroused in a manner that allows her to temper her boundaries and engage. Stella has numerous concerns, Winston's age being the most pronounced preoccupation for example. Enjoying Winston in Jamaica, Stella returns to her home in San Francisco to the loss of her employment. Feeling "betrayed", she attempts to continue to remain connected to the life she had, yet feels burdened by the transition and instability of her new reality.

When returning to Jamaica with her son and niece to visit Winston, she learns of Delilah's cancer and the dire condition of her prognosis. Visiting Delilah within the hospital and singing "Row, Row, Row Your Boat", Stella pauses upon the lyric, "Life is but a dream", allowing her to recognize the delicacy of the lived experience. Losing a part of herself as an employee and as a mother while being terminated from her job, Stella is able to manage in the absence of demonstrative affect. Then the worst happens for Stella: Delilah dies. When Stella loses Delilah, she vulnerably frequently becomes tearful and appears, for the first time, grief-stricken.

Not all losses are made equal. Some goodbyes are welcomed, whereas with others it is hard even to conceive of their existence. This film illustrates that loss and how humans experience loss are on a continuum. A death may occur over time without our awareness that small aspects are disappearing, even of ourselves. Loss can occur as a consequence of a circumstance (such as a business merger) or suddenly (such as when one is unaware of a loved one's illness). When one has some semblance of control, situations that create comfort can make loss feel less grave. Consequently, when Stella is at risk of losing an additional important aspect of her life, Winston, she finds herself desperately accepting his love and marriage proposal.

Being given the opportunity to be authentic regarding one's loving, libidinal feelings when fearing loss or when loss has occurred can feel like an opportunity of a lifetime. If one does not seize the moment, will one be vulnerable to feelings of regret and predictable sorrow? These passionate pleas to acknowledge the presence of love despite past hurts, betrayals, and disappointments have the possibility to impact one's life indefinitely. What a risk Bleek, Marcus, Darius, and Stella took by exposing their heart so defenselessly. With big love to be gained and large losses to be had, these films support that gambling on love is a bet worth placing.

Legacy Films

There were two extraordinary films within the 1990s that are highlighted as legacy films: *Malcolm X* (1992) and *What's Love Got to Do With It* (1993). As these films both captured the stories of iconic persons in Black history for their differing

64   Death and Rebirth to Evolution (1990–1999)

contributions to the community and the world, these films also fit within the decade of prolific works of other filmmakers addressing trauma and family values.

Malcolm X (1992)

For some, one's life is perceived as being steady and linear with tolerable bumps along the way. This steadiness lacks curves, twists, and devastating hardships. The certainty that one will wake to another day that holds a similar promise of predictability awaits. Though, for others, life is experienced in a manner with less ease. Bumps in the road are characterized by turbulent assaults of aggression that create an unpredictable climate breeding opportunity for trauma. Numbing life and engaging in self-destructive behaviors can manifest as a consequence to these traumatic experiences. The certainty to wake another day and what is expected can be questionable in these environments. For many years, Malcolm Little experienced the latter life experience, though found a path to be reborn. In his wake, he possessed the power to generate an inertia to move people and a community as Malcolm X.

The film *Malcolm X*, based upon the book *The Autobiography of Malcolm X* by Alex Haley and Attallah Shabazz (1989), illustrates the life of Malcolm Little and his journey to becoming the infamous Malcolm X. Detailing Malcolm X's early childhood experiences of violence brought upon by the Ku Klux Klan towards his family, the impact of grief upon the family after his father died, and the ailing mental health of his mother suggests that life for Malcolm Little was accompanied by difficult feelings likely of fear, sadness, and lack. As followed in the book, the film shows Malcolm Little's illicit substance dependency along with his illegal employment that results in a brief incarceration.

Within confinement, Malcolm is introduced to the Nation of Islam and soon reborn as Malcolm X. As a devout practicing Muslim of the Nation of Islam, Malcolm X embarks upon a spiritual journey that manifests in a life of education, advocacy, and activism for the Black community. As time progresses, Malcolm X's ability to remain in alignment with the principles of The Nation of Islam is fractured creating a bifurcation in his relationship with leadership and his spiritual teacher and mentor Elijah Muhammad. Once this rupture occurs, it provides Malcolm X an opportunity to explore Islamic principles upon a spiritual pilgrimage. During this time, he connects to his true desired values. He is also aware that at the conclusion of this trip he must return to the chaos involving his religious home and the curiosities the government has about him.

In concert with the beautiful technical aspects of this film—cinematography, lighting, wardrobe, staging, and score—the audience is able to visually follow the life of a civil rights leader evolving into the individual he became in time, once experiencing a contrasting life prior. Within this decade as earlier explored, stories pertaining to traumatic pasts and present circumstances were prevalent, into which this narrative fit perfectly. Though Malcolm Little experienced hardships, we see that there is healing from his traumatic past. Malcolm X, an individual who

Death and Rebirth to Evolution (1990–1999)   65

regained a sense of himself, works towards becoming his ideal self that included serving, educating, and elevating the community.

Despite the bereft impending conclusion, the film instills the audience with not only an education regarding who Malcolm Little and Malcolm X was, but a hope that everyone is able to return and blossom after a history of trauma. As new challenges were experienced well within his adulthood, Malcolm X's possession of the above values served as consistent protective factors allowing situations that could be experienced as horrifying and debilitating to be successfully defended against and used productively. In particular, Malcolm X is seen using community challenges as opportunities to further educate and instill values of empowerment within his community.

What's Love Got to Do With It (1993)

With the gross depiction of trauma located in film works during the 1990s, *What's Love Got to Do With It* falls naturally within this decade's film collection. Honoring the true story of the life of Anna Mae Bullock, and famously the life of Tina Turner, seemed a timely necessity to document the impact trauma has upon an individual and those around them. By being shown the experience of domestic violence, intimate partner violence (IPV), non-fatal strangulation, substance use, and rape, audiences are possibly able to develop a newfound empathy for those in the captivity of spousal abusive relationships. Though this film was made in 1993, it is important to note that IPV remains disproportionately overrepresented within the Black community. Specifically, within the National Intimate Partner and Sexual Violence Survey (NISVS), 45.1% of Black women reported that they had experienced sexual violence, physical aggression, and/or stalking that had been perpetrated by an intimate partner (Smith et al., 2017). West (2021) reports that these numbers support that over "six million Black women are survivors of some form of IPV during their lifetime" as cited by Black et al. (2011, p. 749).

And, yet, this film has a great source of entertainment. Significant contributions to the film included recollections of the music that was created by Ike and Tina Turner, and dance performances and costumes highlighting 1960s–1980s fashion. Yet, *What's Love Got to Do With It* also offers an account of the variables necessary for an individual to find a way to escape an abusive relationship and maintain that safety once secured. Rediscovering oneself, experiencing love for self that manifests in respecting oneself, locating inner strength, and experiencing the fatigue of being victimized coupled with the stronger urge to grasp libidinal drives to live bring one to lack further tolerance for the circumstances of today, and, in turn, to begin to fight to have a safe tomorrow. Though research is lacking in understanding protective factors that Black women possess that demonstrate their resilience, higher levels of spirituality and greater social support account for a few protective factors (Howell et al., 2018). Similarly, Tina Turner emerges reborn in new faith, love for herself, and a desire to share who she has become with others through song. Her life in the absence of IPV and trauma reflects what is coined as post-traumatic growth, where an individual engages in making meaning of the violence and experiences "transformative changes in an individual's perceptions of self, others and life" (Mushonga et al., 2021, p. 153; Tedeschi & Calhoun, 2004).

The films that were explored within this decade do not capture all of the important films of the 1990s. Rather, this exploration provides a view of how an assortment of what were greenlit for box office features contributed to the manner in which we view and perceive African Americans, how we navigate this world, self, and others. These films call into question, do my specific defensive mechanisms work to serve me best? As the sheer number of films featuring African American individuals in leading roles grew exponentially from the 1980s to the 1990s, we approach the 2000s and years thereafter with greater exposure to African American narratives, idiosyncratic characters, and their psychology within film.

4

Dreams Come True (2000–2009)

The 2000s continued on the trajectory of crafting cinematic classics. Though less prolific within this decade, it did not in any manner diminish the impact African American films had upon their viewers. This decade heralded themes that were meaningful and depicted evolution in what audiences were interested in screening. Such themes were, in essence, emotionally lighter, with an illustration of hope for dreams actualized and societal awareness.

To examine this decade thoroughly, we must include a prominent character that was present in a myriad of Black films within this decade. Ever present in the box office, this character was enjoyed by individuals across generations where people relate to her as a peer, mother, aunt, grandmother, or a family member most families have. Madea within Tyler Perry's productions (performed by Tyler Perry), whether within minute moments or holding a lead role in feature films, was hailed as a comedic contribution to the entertainment world. Madea depicted wisdom, nurturance, love, and had an abundance of spunk. The ten films that tend to be referred to as "Madea films" and the additional films where she is present as a supporting character are not reviewed in psychological nuance within this book. As such, the impact this character had is noted, for to omit the presence of this role would not acknowledge a significant body of work that has been meaningful for the African American community.

Within a *60 Minutes* episode transcript Tyler Perry's films were described as "guaranteed box office gold" due to his successful ability to appeal to "his devoted audience: largely African-American, church-going, working class and female" (Pitts, in Streeter, 2009). This source concurred that "long ignored by Hollywood, they [Tyler's audience] come to see something they can't get anywhere else: inspirational stories about people like themselves, and to laugh at characters like his 'Madea', the wise-cracking grandmother". Perry reported:

> Madea is a cross between my mother and my aunt. She's the type of grandmother that was on every corner when I was growing up. … She smoked. She walked out of the house with her curlers and her muumuu and she watched everybody's kids. She didn't take no crap. She's a strong figure where I come from. In my part of the African-American community. And I say that because I'm sure

DOI: 10.4324/9781003399902-5

that there are some other parts of the African-American community that may be looking at me now going, "Who does he think he's speaking of?" But, for me, this woman was very, very visible. (Perry, in Streeter, 2009)

The patterns highlighted for these films offered audiences a predictable multi-hour performance. When screening a film with Madea, "you're always gonna see a person of faith. Nine times out of ten, it'll be a woman who has problems, who has lost faith or lost her way", Perry explained (in Streeter, 2009). "There's always gonna be a moment of redemption somewhere for someone".

"And then there are the grittier, darker elements: the violence, especially directed at women and children, sex and child abuse, prostitution, and drugs use. But there is always a fairy tale ending, a happy marriage, a reconciliation—often delivered with a dose of Gospel music" (Pitts, in Streeter, 2009). And though Madea films have been box office successes, "there are some who don't understand Perry's work and dismiss it, many of them African Americans. They find characters like Madea and Mr. Brown demeaning caricatures, racial stereotypes" (Pitts, in Streeter, 2009). Such audiences are concerned or embarrassed, which suggests that Perry's work that includes Madea is moving the country backwards rather than forwards. Whether one agrees with this hypothesis or does not, we cannot ignore that Madea approaches sensitive topics that challenge others around her to gain greater insight into their behaviors and motivations. She broaches topics of forgiveness, self-protection from abuses, family, personal values, faith, and love in a manner that holds compassion and is confrontational many times with humor—and, when needed, with a warmth that offers comfort at the most difficult emotional times. In her wisdom, she is not a perfect Christian woman. She frequently flirts with law enforcement and presents at court appearances to plead her cases as depicted in several films where she regales her religious affiliation as a way to show her developed remorse. She can be benevolent, stand up for others—mostly family—under any circumstances, and is a source of support who speaks candidly in the absence of her audience's desired censor. When she sees that someone requires her support, is hurting, or is struggling to make decisions that are within good health, Madea advocates on that person's behalf selfishly as a protector, even in the face of making her a bully perpetrator and at risk of committing a crime. As this character is consistent—thus, predictable—she holds a great deal of richness in the complex and at times contradictory aspects of Madea's personality and subsequent behaviors exhibited.

Audiences for two decades have had mixed feelings regarding who Madea has been for themselves and others. Perry's commitment to depicting the character Madea both welcomed audiences to conceptualize life situations in different ways while asserting in Hollywood that there indeed are people like Madea who exist in this world.

Further, Legacy Films sharing the visual narratives of *Antwone Fisher* (2002), *Ray* (2004), and *The Great Debaters* (2007) are discussed. Similarly, as previous decades reveal, legacy films tend to share themes present in fiction films of the

Dreams Come True (2000–2009)   69

same decade. Without difference, these legacy films highlight dreams held that appear unattainable and dreams that are accomplished through dedication, clarity of mind and heart, and through commitment.

Love and Basketball (2000)

Home is one of the most prominent symbols of one's self and allows for one's interior psyche to be represented in one's exterior environment. *Love and Basketball* follows the life of Monica (performed by Sanaa Latham), a young girl who is committed to developing her basketball skills as a child. Once her family relocates into a new neighborhood, she meets her neighbor Quincy (acted by Omar Epps), who is equally interested in basketball. When they play one another while she wears nongendered clothing and a baseball cap low over her face, he finds that not only are her skills superior to his, but she is also a girl. Over the years, they form a friendship with one another that frequently resembles a sibling relationship.

As they mature, they develop an intimate relationship with one another. They challenge one another and are supportive of one another. However, when Quincy learns that his father, a professional basketball player, has had sexual indiscretions that lead to the end of his marriage with his mother, he places Monica in an unthinkable position: to choose to comfort him or make the curfew that her basketball coach has enforced to prepare for the following day's game. Monica makes the difficult decision to choose her obligations to the team and her desires to play, with the promise of being emotionally available to Quincy at a different time. At the time of decision making, Monica, like many, does not make a conscious offense to neglect the needs of their loved one. Competing demands created an environment where Quincy's emotional comfort was not provided—an act that was not committed out of her lack of care for him, yet made to place the care of herself as paramount. As a result, it is not always clear that one's decisions are creating a rupture that will shift the trajectory of a relationship, and, specifically, in a direction undesired.

Consequent to Monica's decision, Quincy was unable to forgive her for not being there in the manner he needed. Rather than communicate the pain he felt by her abandonment, Quincy presented as emotionally guarded relying upon the defense mechanisms of both avoidance and acting out to demonstrate the pain he experienced that night. Evading her inquiries regarding his emotional state and appearing guarded allowed him to protect himself from further injury from Monica. Due to Quincy's inability to move past the rupture between the two of them, he terminated the relationship leaving Monica with regret.

"In an effort to reduce feelings of disappointment and regret, one may take action and attempt to understand their responsibility for the unsuccessful situation" (Marshall Woods, 2018, p. 49). "Regretful experiences can have a tremendous impact on one's personal self, one's family, and social relations alike" (Marshall Woods, 2018, p. 49). Monica finds herself, for approximately five years, tending to questions such as *"What could have been different? Could I have said something to have changed the situation?"*, questions that Roese and Summerville (2005)

70 Dreams Come True (2000–2009)

report frequently occurs. Within *Best Psychology in Film* (2018), the following passage that with great similarity describes the experience of Troy Maxson in the film *Fences* equally describes Monica's positioning within this film:

> "Regret, I began to realize, is delicately and dramatically poised between hope and despair" (DeMarco, 2015, p. 55). It is an unpleasant, counterfactual, self-focused emotion that results from having made an unfavorable choice (Joel et al., 2012, p. 348). Regret arises "from a comparison between an actual outcome and a better outcome that might have occurred had another option been chosen" (Marcatto & Ferrante, 2008, p. 87). Sadness and hurt ensues, and feelings of disappointment and discomfort remain active. Regret can have a shelf life of a lifetime, where "unalleviated regret is a terrible thing. It is sorrow caused by actions in the past that are beyond one's power to remedy" (DeMarco, 2015, p. 56).

Despite the years moving forward, Monica is unable to feel a sense of wholeness in Quincy's absence. Though becoming employed to play women's basketball abroad, she articulates her displeasure in playing because something is missing, which she articulates as, "It's you, you're missing" to Quincy when he inquires. Monica finds herself articulating to Quincy that she is aware she could have done differently in the relationship at that time, suggesting a great deal of introspection and reflection had occurred over the years. Though, Quincy owns his part, and notes that the demise of the relationship was not only due to Monica's choices. In fact, he recognized he began to have unresolved trust issues when his father committed adultery. Despite this, Monica takes her literal and figurative shot to regain Quincy's love by playing a game of basketball for his heart in love.

Love and Basketball is a film that depicts Monica in a search to find herself and her emotional home that is lost when the love of Quincy is lost. In the absence of this emotional home coupled with regret, she terminates her notoriety as a famous basketball player in Spain, takes a job as a banker in her father's branch, and attempts to have a life in the absence of basketball. At the conclusion of the game with Quincy, Monica was finally able to become complete in the manner she craved, enabling her to achieve her dream of playing women's basketball in the United States and return to her emotional home in the love of Quincy.

Drumline (2002)

The dream of matriculating college to further one's education may be considered a quotidian desire in the United States. Yet, with the cost that is accrued in attending higher education, there are many who sacrifice their dream due to a lack of means and opportunity. The talented drummer, Devon (performed by Nick Cannon), finds that his dream can indeed be actualized when offered a full music scholarship to pursue higher education while playing in the university's band entering the drumline. However, Devon's first year of university lends itself to lessons that are not only academic and music related. Rather, within spaces of small and large groups and intimate interactions, Devon is positioned in an environment to learn more regarding himself and others.

Devon presents as a confident youngster, an arrogant, entitled young man. When one is confident, according to Merriam-Webster's dictionary, one possesses "a feeling or consciousness of one's powers or of reliance on one's circumstances" (Merriam-Webster 2024b). The person has a "faith or belief that one will act in a right, proper or effective way" and there is "the quality or state of being certain" (2024b). However, Devon's arrogance as defined as "an attitude of superiority manifested in an overbearing manner or in presumptuous claims or assumptions" (Merriam-Webster 2024a), coupled with the enactment of entitlement, "the right to benefits specified especially by law or contract" and "belief that one is deserving of or entitled to certain privileges" (Merriam-Webster 2024c), led him to behave in ways that garnered unpleasant consequences. Devon's behaviors many times made it difficult for him to be open to learning in ways that would nurture his global sense of self as well as his talents as a drummer.

Interpersonally, individuals had numerous reactions to Devon's arrogance and entitlement. At the onset of the film, his mother is found cheering in pride regarding his academic success of graduating from high school and playing the school song with his bandmates. Under Devon's self-appointed leadership, as the students performed, he encouraged his peers to change the tempo of the school song from its prescribed arrangement. This action resulted in the teacher shifting the remaining students to match Devon's suggestion and performing the song as Devon wished without consequence from the band leader nor his mother at the conclusion.

Once arriving to the university presenting in a similar arrogant manner, his bandmate Sean (performed by Leonard Roberts) despised his behaviors. As the band carried the mission, "One band, one sound", Devon's desire to be a soloist and proceed in an independent way led Sean to confront him and investigate who Devon was musically. Sean's investigation can be seen as conflictual. In particular, whereas some would suggest Sean's energy towards creating a credible way to expose Devon as a neophyte was based in envy, the desire to possess what one has with the equal desire to see another person damaged or destroyed, others may suggest that Sean was protecting the band from a person who struggled with teamwork. Both can and seem equally to be true. This polarization of Sean's character, where he is both a protector of the band and musicianship while being someone who is willing to destroy, adds to the richness of the dynamic had between Devon and himself.

Ultimately, Sean's preoccupation with Devon led to discoveries that caused Devon to experience the negative consequence of being temporarily exiled from the band. Rather than use the consequence as an opportunity, Devon's initial response was to terminate his membership with the band which also jeopardized his academic financial supports. However, once Devon was exposed and desired to remediate areas of weakness, Sean's envy began to dissipate. In response, Devon and Sean were better able to collaborate with one another. Devon's ability to shed his arrogance and entitlement and humble himself allowed him to arrive to the destination he desired, in a position of leadership.

Hustle and Flow (2005)

> "This is important now, this is serious. Look at me… Shit, everyone gotta have a dream".
>
> Skinny Black (performed by Ludacris)

DJay (performed by Terrence Howard) is an individual employed as a drug dealer and negotiates sex for the women "in his care". He refers to himself as a "pimp" and the care that he provides the women includes housing, encouragement when needed to move "the product" (sexual favors), and substances to facilitate the ease of their participation. Within this role, DJay is shown to have characteristics and behave in manners that are polarizing. He is both ruthless and caring, a liar and a truth-teller. With the financial limitations and stress of being a hustler, DJay begins to examine his life in his forties feeling that he may be having a "midlife crisis".

The life exploration creates significant distress for DJay. He explicitly wonders whether the life that he has is all life has to offer. He is reminded of his talents in his youth for rapping, and is reminded constantly on television of a successful rapper, Skinny Black, from his hometown who made it mainstream. As DJay watches this rapper's content, he lights up with childish excitement, soliciting the women who are employed by him and reside in his home to watch as he views his media. As he and this rapper share the same high school and age range, DJay begins to suggest that he has a legitimate connection with this rapper, which leads him to gain the faith of a high school classmate working as a sound engineer and his colleague in producing music on his behalf—supporting his dream. As these men are equally unfulfilled with their lives' employment and mediocre financial success, they are inspired by DJay and work committedly to fulfill not only his dreams, yet what becomes their dream as well.

Grit, determination, persistence, and desperation cultivate an environment where creation and production become the sole focus of the home. Despite receiving support from the women whom he employs, DJay experiences vitriol from Lexus (acted by Paula Jai Parker). Her disillusionment in DJay coupled with the frustration she has for her life circumstance creates an emotional volcano that erupts frequently. Within any situation, her upset bubbles to the surface where her lava hits not only DJay but innocent, uninvolved individuals such as DJay's producer's wife and infant son. Due to her relentless inability to engage in a positive manner, DJay rids his home of the poison which she brings. This behavior has its casualties, as both she and her son find themselves homeless and on the street. From this perspective Lexus appears toxic and resentful; and, there is no perspective that makes her character otherwise. Yet, this character displays the stereotypical woman, specifically, the Sapphire, who is disgruntled and people question why and how one can behave in such a manner. Due to her supporting role and the attention called to rooting for DJay in his endeavors, it becomes easy to label her character as a hater, and the one that attempts to get in the way of a dream being actualized. Rather, it is also easy to evade that she is a mother in a codependent relationship of both being supported by and supporting her pimp, where it is insinuated that she experiences physically abusive violent interactions with others. Why might she lack the ability to be a constant delight? And, when she is displaced from her home, the home that she financially supports through her employment at a strip club and sexual favors she provides, when viewed in the theaters, audiences provided sounds supporting the cruelty she experienced. This depiction of Lexus allows a both/and situation to be beautifully illustrated. Lexus is indeed emotionally toxic and her departure from her environment with her son, for all involved, seemed to be a healthy decision. Yet, Lexus as a human and a financial contributor to the household warranted respect that she was not readily provided. These two existing realities created a cycle for Lexus leaving emanating upset, hurt, and disbelief that her reality under the current circumstances could be better. Pointedly, Lexus became unable to relate to the individuals in the household due to her inability to believe that it was possible for a dream of a different life to become a reality.

Further, there was an additional character that was depicted in a similar light. Nola (acted by Taryn Manning), a prostitute who works for DJay, carries an equal level of restlessness. She is acutely aware that the life that she has does not support what she desires. Yet, dissimilar to DJay and the others, when asked, Nola is unable to identify what she wants. This lack of specific self-awareness in the presence of her awareness of knowing that her reality is not desired creates an emotional conflict for Nola. Her acknowledgment that she desired different makes her relatable and respectful of others' pursuits of dreams. In an effort to assuage her anxieties, DJay provides her the narrative that she "is in charge". Despite knowing that this narrative is false, as she is a prostitute in an employment relationship with a pimp, Nola allows DJay at times to "mess with my head, because sometimes it needs messing with". Nola appears to struggle with challenges in knowing herself and therefore self-doubt cloaks her. This self-doubt "reflect[s] one's feeling of uncertainty about competence" and also manifests in her understanding of her self-worth (Zhao & Wichman, 2015, p. 1). However, throughout the film, Nola begins to advocate for her freedom of choice, that she must have a say in what behaviors she will enact and with whom pertaining to the employment agreement she has with DJay. And though it never becomes clear within the film what Nola's independent dream may be, she adopts the one DJay ascribes to her, that she is in fact in charge. As a result of her adoption of this role, she experiences success and a moment of fulfillment in moving the needle forward for DJay and his production team.

This family that is built of dreamers find a way to support one another's future success. Despite the challenges faced, they remain able to utilize their personal talents (rapping, sound engineering, music production, singing, and project management) to contribute to the success of all.

Dreamgirls (2006)

Regardless of whether dreams are taken away or stolen, the mass of hurt and pain makes for a barren terrain, where the light of life is unable to be visible. Within the film *Dreamgirls*, the characters all had similar dreams of becoming and furthering their careers as performers making it with mainstream audiences. At the onset, the characters are present to perform, competing for the prize of being showcased for one week at a local club. Numerous local singing groups perform; and, specifically, the Dreamettes, three young women, desire their first break. Though the contest is fixed with a predetermined winner, the Dreamettes are introduced to Curtis Taylor Jr. (acted by Jamie Foxx), who offers an opportunity for them to sing backup for a performer, Mr. James "Thunder" Early (performed by Eddie Murphy). This collusion of talent leads to love, deceit, betrayals, fame, and heartbreak.

Effie (acted by Jennifer Hudson), the lead of the Dreamettes, possessed a striking voice. Once the group was able to establish themselves and to headline, the Dreamettes became mature and were referred to as the Dreamgirls. In this stage, Deena Jones (depicted by Beyoncé Knowles) was instructed that she would be made to sing lead in hopes that her "lighter sound" would allow for greater crossover into the White market. Leaving Effie feeling rejected and questioning how she physically appeared to her lover, Curtis Taylor, Effie's attempt to advocate for her dream of being lead was quelled when her family constructed of her groupmates, brother, and manager convinced her by reminding her that the dream held was not only for her, but for everyone. They assured her that their dream could become a reality if she relented—convincing her that indeed she should remain committed; to stop now would be to the detriment of all of their success.

As the young women settle into their roles, Effie grows restless in her position singing backup. During a recording, she takes a predominate stance, and uses her voice to overpower her group. She finds herself no longer able to remain in her place in the back despite her group begging her to do so. She reiterates that Deena has stolen her dream and struggles to be in a position that is accompanied by such great discomfort.

As most performing groups are portrayed within these musicals, *Dreamgirls* has a similar tale. Following the group's success breaking into the main markets, experiencing love with colleagues, engaging in extramarital affairs on the road, substance use, overdose, and death while placed in the context of the various societal movements of its time, *Dreamgirls* entertains in scores. Yet, what is also gleaned is that when someone loses their dreams or they are stolen, there is a death that occurs. The chase for the dream to return, excitement for its potential, and feelings of defeat when it is unable to be actualized create an incommensurable grief that escapes reason and leaves a desire to extinguish the disappointment that the dream may be lost forever. Similarly, James Early experienced such a pain when his music no longer touched audiences in the way it had in the past and his manager no longer desired to invest in his talents. After experiencing defeat when his performance of a heartfelt, timely song in a society full of conflict and war was rejected, he looked to soothe his injured ego in the manner to which he became accustomed, with illicit substances.

For Effie, her lost dream resulted in similar, yet less bleak horizons. Becoming a single parent and unemployed because, "All I know how to do is sing" left her in a walk-up apartment, relying upon public assistance and lacking confidence in herself. Her defeats continued to mount when a song which she recorded with her brother's writing talents began to create traction and was stolen by the performing group she once belonged to. This experience adds further injury to Effie, as the perpetrators of her career dreams continue to assault and place her in a position of lack.

Dreamgirls leaves with a happy ending, a reunion for the women, who are able to come to a mutual respect for one another at the conclusion of their career with one another. Reunions are also present for their former manager when he learns he has a daughter conceived with Effie. It is not uncommon to hear encouragements that if you have a dream, pursue it with strength and might. The film *Dreamgirls* suggests that the nurturing of one's dream is paramount in the success of cultivating one's ability to freely live.

Stomp the Yard (2007)

There are times when one lacks having a specific vision and arrives at a predetermined dream to engage. DJ (performed by Columbus Short) finds himself living the dream of his brother to attend college. DJ and his younger brother were portrayed at the onset of the film as close, sharing a similar interest in dance. Their talents allowed them to have a group of individuals who danced with them to compete in dance challenges at local clubs. Upon a win one night, the team that lost the challenge confronted the group demanding the money that was won. When a scuffle ensued, DJ's brother, Duron (acted by Chris Brown), was shot and died. While it was Duron's dream to pursue higher education in university, DJ is removed from his home town and placed into university near his aunt and uncle's home in what appears to be a way to reform him and a way to ensure his safety.

Within DJ's college experience, he becomes exposed to the culture of fraternities and sororities. Initially, he does not perceive the benefits of being a part of Greek life; rather, he misunderstands such organizations and holds a contemptuous confusion for them and the people within them. DJ's response to Greek life is not surprising based upon his presentation. Specifically, he presents as an individual who is self-involved and views independence as necessary. Collaboration with others is minimized and dismissed. He functions with a baseline level of skepticism and intolerance. In particular, and strikingly, his self-involvement results in being grossly competitive, being only concerned with winning even at the expense of others who are supportive friends. It is only with the disappointment of him and his friends losing a competition as a direct result of his unwillingness to work as part of a team that DJ truly reconsiders his approach of pursuing goals alone.

In fairness, in understanding DJ it is important to hold in mind that, though not referred to in the film frequently, this character may remain bereft. The length of time between his brother's death and his arrival to matriculate in university is not stated, yet the time between incidences appears brief. Not only may DJ have been grieving the loss of his brother, but Cameron (2008) reports that siblings also may suffer decreased functioning of their parents' parenting as a result of their own grief. As a result, it can be wondered whether his selfishness was a result of fear of becoming close to another individual, having lost his brother and potentially the emotional availability of his parent(s). It can be questioned whether the idea of a brotherhood of any type was threatening as he knew full well what it would feel like to lose another brother. Further, navigating a new environment in grief may have further fostered his feelings of being alone and unrelatable. As a result, DJ's challenges with acculturation to campus life became multi-tiered. In particular, he never envisioned himself in a higher education environment and was uncertain how to navigate the culture. The culture he was presented with was one that appeared idyllic—greenery on the quad, well-manicured buildings and lawns (ones he helped keep under his uncle's supervision), and brotherhoods and sisterhoods of like-minded individuals that displayed respect for one another—and was very different from the club and dirt road traversed where he found himself at the onset of the film before his brother was killed. Being sent to university at this time, albeit alone in his grief, may have provided him with safety from his neighborhood where it was proven fatal violence was present, as well as a way to shelter him from the grief of his parents.

Adopting someone else's dream can feel inauthentic. Ideally, being open to the riches that await an unimagined journey will lead to connections and love that foster one to become a version of oneself that was never dreamt could be possible. DJ's experience living his brother's desires offered him a unique opportunity that culminated in exceeding his personal expectations while exposing his true potential.

Legacy Films

Antwone Fisher (2002)

As previous films within this decade highlight the importance of having a dream, many portrayed desires pertaining to careers, achievement of fame, and having one's voice heard. The film *Antwone Fisher* depicts the real-life experience of Antwone Fisher (acted by Derek Luke), an individual whose dreams are perhaps more simplistic and endearing in quality—yet, with great potential to be fulfilling. The film opens with Antwone sharing a dream he had from which he quickly awakes. This dream depicts a home Antwone walks into, with a welcoming family surrounding abundance in the form of love and a cornucopia of food awaiting him. And as most dreams in persons' lives take time to achieve, have their challenges and moments of hopelessness, and require perseverance, Antwone Fisher's life narrative is not shy of the same ingredients. This autobiographical film that shares horrors he experienced both as a child and as a young man, leaving trauma to contend with in his early adulthood years, is a tear-jerker with its inspiring ending allowing a great deal of psychodynamic contemplative nuance in between.

Antwone is introduced as an individual who questions his safety. Within his foster home, Antwone is physically and emotionally abused by his primary caregiver.

He is constantly told that he is unwanted, unlovable, and lacks the worthiness of being honored as a distinct individual. Mrs. Tate (performed by Novella Nelson) had three boys in her care including Antwone. She utilized systemic racism such as colorism to create fissures within the relationships the children cultivated with one another, ensuring they remained feeling alone and unable to trust and feel a sense of emotional safety. Her stripping of their identities by her unwillingness to refer to them by name, but rather use of a different tone of voice to distinguish each from one another while referring to them all as a demeaning epithet, further created an environment void of psychologically and emotionally healthy nurturance.

Additionally, Antwone's safety was further compromised by Mrs. Tate's adult niece who repeatedly sexually molested him. Her advances that were hostile and aggressive, characterized by both physical and sexual assaults, created significant distress and allowed for no reprieve when Mrs. Tate was away from the home. Antwone fantasizes about a simpler time, where he is loved by his family and feels safe. Alternatively, it is portrayed that the young Antwone lives in a perpetual state of unsafety due to these consistently inflicted traumas. Possessing an environment of safety and love seems only attainable in his subconscious mind during his slumber.

In response to his inability to process his traumatic history, Antwone fights. He demonstrates to the world how he feels emotionally within his inner self: conflicted. A result of Antwone's aggressive behavior towards his superior Navy officer provides him an opportunity to receive three sessions of psychotherapy to begin to explore the etiology of his behaviors and how to craft ways to cope with life's situations. Antwone is introduced to Dr. Davenport (acted by Denzel Washington), a navy psychiatrist who performs his work with compassion, curiosity, and love. As mental health professionals may have many thoughts, feelings, and hesitations regarding the use of the word "love" as it relates to one's patient, this sentiment is explicitly stated within the film, rather than implied. It becomes understood that Dr. Davenport's love for Antwone is based upon his identification with Antwone. Though Dr. Davenport's behaviors and manner appear opposite to Antwone's (i.e. he is calm, slow to upset, and rational), he is also a man in pain treating a patient in similar pain. They both share the history of losing family; whereas Antwone is unfamiliar with his biological family, Dr. Davenport learns that he and his wife are unable to conceive and have the family he so desired. These characters are mirrors of one another, both grieving men, one grieving the past and the other grieving their desired future. While both men are bereft, Antwone externalizes by using physical aggression whereas Dr. Davenport internalizes by using withdrawal and isolation of affect. These men exhibit polarized ways of navigating their grief, yet experienced the same outcomes: strained interpersonal relationships. Dr. Davenport is keenly aware that Antwone has the power to connect with his family and have an optimum outcome in comparison to what he imagines of his own circumstances; thus he encourages him to find his family of origin.

Unger's (2013) research supports the finding that in order to mend from trauma, one must belong to a community that supports such healing. Antwone finds such a

78   Dreams Come True (2000–2009)

community, albeit small to begin with: only friendly coworkers, a psychiatrist, and a female companion who eases his way. With the help, hope, and love of them, Antwone is able to obtain his dream in reality: finding his family who welcomes him in love.

Ray (2004)

The life of Ray Charles is one that was epic, with abundant human greatness and its challenges. The film *Ray* follows the life of Ray Charles (acted by Jamie Foxx) from his younger years until late into his musical career. He is introduced living in a humble home with his mother and younger brother in Florida. As a young boy, he proves to be a gifted piano player. Within these tender years, Ray also experiences a devastating trauma where he witnesses the drowning of his brother in a basin for washing. Later, specifically at the age of seven, his vision begins to fail him and he ultimately becomes blind. His mother, Aretha (performed by Sharon Warren), shares with him her desire for him to be able to navigate the world independently, never requiring assistance from others, for she did not wish for him to be inhibited by his lack of sight. Within the film, her love was shown towards him abundantly as she successfully prepared him for the world in the manner she could. As Ray ages, he matriculates at a school for the deaf and blind to become better equipped at navigating the world.

As the film progresses, Mr. Charles' trauma concerning his brother's death becomes evident. At the time of the incident, as a young Ray, he stands frozen as he watches his brother fall into the basin where he is unable to free himself. Unable to move, by the time his mother comes outside, his brother is taken out of the water lifeless. His mother asks why he had not alerted her, and Ray remains in place, silent. Over time, and upon his travels on The Chitlin' Circuit promoting his music, he is portrayed being knowledgeable that his bandmates utilized substances and asked for them to share them with him. As substance use can be abused as a means to evoke the defense mechanism of escapism, one can begin to question, what is Mr. Charles escaping exactly?

Despite Mr. Charles' profound musical success, he experiences symptoms that suggest his original trauma and associated feelings of grief and guilt impacted his overall functioning. The Diagnostic and Statistical Manual of Mental Disorders, Fifth Edition, Text Revision notes that a person struggles with a mental health concern when there exists impairment that negatively affects one's interpersonal and professional/academic functioning. Mr. Charles' heroin usage strained his marital relationship and caused him to become unreliable professionally. Specifically for Mr. Charles, his addiction created challenges in his marital union while his wife was pregnant. Having affairs with two of his backup singers caused strife and provoked one to leave the band. Individuals interested in working with him became concerned regarding his behaviors, as they were aware of his substance use. After some time, his substance use also resulted in arrests where he was court-mandated to undergo substance rehabilitation. With the above in concert, Mr. Charles demonstrates an individual in need of healing and recovery.

During rehabilitation, Mr. Charles experiences visions in which he sees his deceased brother and mother. His brother shares with Mr. Charles that his death was not his fault and his mother, albeit proud of his accomplishments and success, shares her disappointment that in fact his addiction has made him dependent in a manner that she did not desire for him. Within the film, this experience is equally confrontational and compassionate. Mr. Charles is asked to contend with the fact that he is both the punisher and the punished by his addiction, both the aggressor and the victim. With this knowledge, it becomes clear that he has the power to free himself from the pain that he better understands is self-inflicted.

The Great Debaters (2007)

In 1935, Professor Tolson (acted by Denzel Washington) inspired students matriculating at Wiley College, a Historically Black College located in Marshall, Texas, to develop the university's first debate team. Attempting to establish itself to be recognized as a competitive debate team, this group of students and Professor Tolson traveled through the South to various Historically Black Colleges and Universities (HBCUs) debating and remaining undefeated. Engaging in a home-grown campaign to market the team's success with predominately White academic institutions, Wiley College's debate team was afforded the opportunity to debate the debate team of the most prestigious university, Harvard College in Cambridge, Massachusetts. Providing compelling arguments, the Wiley College debate team defeated Harvard's team leading to a ten-year undefeated legacy. *The Great Debaters*, based upon the history of success of Wiley College's debate team, proves to be an inspirational underdog tale with its undercurrents exploring the presence and overcoming of the human condition of shame.

"Shame is a negative, crisis emotion closely connected with disgrace" (Scheff, 2000, p. 97). It is an affective experience that evokes one to self-reflect on one's choices and behaviors and in retrospect hold complex multilayered feelings. An individual with the ability to experience shame must be able to self-criticize one's behaviors and possess a "sophisticated self-consciousness" where one is able to recognize that there is a "discrepancy of his/her own assumptions about his/her actual action or state" (Dost & Yagmurlu, 2008, p. 110). Events that render shame are those that hit hard and shake one's self-concept, fostering self-evaluation and causing one to contemplate whether "I am a bad person" (Tangney et al., 2014, p. 799) for choices and decisions made.

Poignant, evocative scenes within *The Great Debaters* depict characters' experience of shame. These scenes are pivotal in highlighting the life of African Americans in the South at that time. The frequency of displays of shame-ridden moments is perhaps reflective of the felt experience of African Americans living under Jim Crow laws. Two scenes explored below offered viewers the impact shame can have upon how one views oneself and others, and the ability it has to create shifts within relationships.

Scene I: On a typical day, Dr. James Farmer, Sr. (acted by Forest Whitaker) was driving his family to town. As White children ran after the car on the side of the road, it caused an alarm when everyone heard a thump under the car. When Dr. Farmer, Sr. investigated, he found he had struck a hog causing its demise. The owners of the pig, two White men, ran to the car and began to threaten Dr. Farmer, Sr. by brandishing a gun. His family watched the men dismiss Dr. Farmer, Sr's. apology and require him to pay for the pig. Dr. Farmer, Sr. agreed to endorse his pay to compensate for the dead hog. Rather than take the check from his hands, the man drops the check and insists that Dr. Farmer, Sr. pick it up. His family, watching from the car, witnesses her husband, their father, a man, be whittled into a subservient role. Humiliated, Dr. Farmer, Sr. returns to the vehicle, physically unscathed with his family physically safe. Yet, emotionally, the family and specifically his son, Jr. (James Farmer, Jr., acted by Denzel Whitaker), are forever scarred by the shame of Dr. Farmer, Sr.'s behaviors that day. Later, Dr. Farmer, Sr. is confronted by Jr. regarding the shame that he believes his father should carry for the events that took place with the owners of the hog. Metcalf (2000) notes, "Shame is ugly ... and being ugly, shame is something we avoid and look at only wincingly. Why is shame painful in this way?" (p. 3). Similarly, unable to look at his father directly, Jr.'s hurt and disappointment conveyed during the confrontation made greater fury ensue. By both parties holding steadfast, an undeniable wedge was created. Jr., now ashamed of his father's choices and behaviors, perceived his father as in a position of being subservient, falling from the pulpit he typically witnessed his father to occupy.

Scene II: The debaters and Professor Tolson were commuting to visit a fellow university for a debate. In transport, they arrived to a mob of children, women, and men watching the burning of a lynched Black man over flames. Professor Tolson advised that the students lie down against the floorboards of the car. The students complied. When the mob identified that the passengers were of color, the mob ran after the car, throwing objects at the windshield and puncturing the glass as the car was successfully able to speed away. Within the final debate, Jr. is called to debate the competitive team from Harvard University, sharing with a captive audience the realities and horrors of lynchings in the South, and recounts their experience. Being in a vulnerable circumstance of survival while lacking agency and personal integrity over the outcome of the experience is shared by Jr. in his final argument, exposing that the burden of shame is carried forever as a consequence of witnessing such heinous assaults.

These moments imbided with shame offered a powerful juxtaposition of the success that the debaters achieved. They are evocative scenes that underscore the nature of the experience these debaters and other individuals of color endured. To understand that to be alive is different than to be safe is a lesson Jr. learns within both scenes examined above. Having Jr., a fourteen year old, in the emerging adult world with college students makes this character uniquely intelligent, yet also naïve and tender for lessons that will ultimately age and mature him. Consequently, he becomes the bearer of truth, acknowledging the inherent shame that arises as a result of being victimized by racism.

5
Unchained... Freedom (2010–2019)

Unlike in previous years, in the 2010s playwrights' theater works were made into feature films allowing for a greater audience to be exposed to plays that were both historical and meaningful. Films such as *Fences* (2016) and *For Colored Girls* (2010) were examples of films created that emulated fictional theater scripts and in many ways when viewing them one felt as if one were in the theater house rather than watching a screen. Globally across the decade, films contained a common theme of challenging the concept of freedom. What does it mean to be free? What are the various types of freedom? How does freedom and the lack of freedom impact one personally and how one may present in social spaces? Freedom within society, freedom in understanding oneself, freedom from standards and stereotypes were all considered within these prolific years. Pursuing freedom in the present day and looking back as to what the pursuit of freedom looked like historically were vulnerably presented.

It is important to mention that films within this decade will be equally examined as in previous chapters with some exceptions. *Fences* (2016), *Moonlight* (2016), and the legacy film *Hidden Figures* (2016) were recognized by nominations among the Academy of Motion Pictures Arts and Sciences. These films as well as the characters in the films that were nominated for Best Actor, Best Actress, and Best Supporting Actress or Actor are discussed in detail in the publication *Best Psychology in Film* (Marshall Woods, 2018). Within those chapters, one will find a dialogue regarding the films' global themes as well as psychodynamic formulations of the characters that were nominated based upon psychological theory that accompany each section. Thus, rather than reiterating such ideas in this space, we may use *Best Psychology in Film* as an auxiliary agent when reviewing this decade in this chapter.

Lastly, Legacy Films throughout the decades within African American film have cinematically illustrated familiar stories documenting historical events while shining a light on stories that have been less recognized. The impossibility of featuring each film was most glaring when conceptualizing the works of this decade. Particularly, this decade produced artworks that highlighted the abundant historical contributions of numerous pioneers. Due to the number of legacy films, the discussion of a film's accuracy by journalists and critic reviews increased with vigor.

DOI: 10.4324/9781003399902-6

Fences (2016)

Please find upon pages 33–64 in *Best Psychology in Film* (Marshall Woods, 2018).

Moonlight (2016)

Please find upon pages 247–277 in *Best Psychology in Film* (Marshall Woods, 2018).

Get Out (2017)

Frederick Douglass (1852) stated, "it is wrong to make men brutes, to rob them of their liberty, to work them without wages". When enslaved, one loses the freedom to navigate one's environment, loses "the power to do as one pleases", to be free "from physical restraint" and loses "the power of choice" (Merriam-Webster, n.d.). Once liberties are stripped from an individual, a desire for freedom and fleeing the oppression becomes the most salient concern. Remaining within an oppressed relationship has the potential to drive "a wise man mad" (Douglass, 1852). *Get Out*, directed by Jordan Peele, depicts a young man in a fight for his freedom once his liberties and physical integrity become compromised.

Slavery, and similarly, acts of modern slavery (i.e. human trafficking, debt bondage, sexual exploitation, contract slavery, etc.) include the use of a host of similar physical and psychological criteria that fosters one to be able to successfully hold another in captivity. According to Paz-Fuchs (2016), enslaved relationships incorporate the use of "humiliation, ownership of the individual, exploitation of vulnerability, and denial of free choice" as well as provide "sub-standard terms and conditions of employment, restrictions on the power to end the employment relationship; and the power to control the worker's life outside the employment relationships" (p. 762). Paz-Fuchs (2016) coined these attributes as the "badges of slavery".

Chris Washington (performed by Daniel Kaluuya) portrays an African American male dating Rose Armitage, a Caucasian female (acted by Allison Williams). The couple is introduced engaging in a loving, playful, intimate relationship. Inviting Chris to meet her parents over a weekend symbolized the trust and commitment that the couple shared. Once arriving to the home, Rose's parents warmly welcomed Chris. Soon after a rapport was built over dinner, Dean Armitage (performed by Bradley Whitford), Rose's father, comments on the obvious, that the people of service to the family, by means of a groundskeeper and housekeeper, were both individuals of color. Speaking to the apparent race dynamics and admitting, "I get it, white family, black servants, it's a total cliché" and offering, "I hate the way it looks", suggested that there was a level of self-awareness, insight, and sensitivity that the family had regarding race. By acknowledging his feelings about the staff, it also served to minimize and assuage possible concerns that there may be unspoken undercurrents of exploitation and racist views that the family held. Despite this notation provided by Mr. Armitage, Chris remained wary of the relations the family had with individuals of color. In response, he began to initiate conversation with the staff in hopes to better understand their relationship with the Armitage family and to apprehend the reason why a single tear rolled down their cheek when they shared their experiences with him.

Detective Sergeant Helen Godos, tactical advisor for the National Crime Agency's modern slavery human trafficking unit, was quoted in *Out of the Shadows* authored by Helen Bird (2017) where she stated, "The message I like to put across is that if it doesn't feel right, it probably isn't" (p. 38); and Chris appeared in agreement. After multiple mysterious events, Chris informed Rose that he wished to leave her family's home which resulted in Rose becoming hurt that he would suggest returning to his home without her. Though being warned to "get out" by an unbeknownst enslaved peer (performed by LaKeith Stanfield), Chris remained committed to Rose, reassuring her that he would not leave, and confessing, "You all I got". Consequently, Chris continued to endure puzzling occurrences and exposure to Rose's charming manipulations, which collectively led him to be vulnerable to becoming the family's next enslaved captive.

As the weekend progressed, Chris learned that his suspicions were warranted. Specifically, he discovered that the family was engaged in enslaving young African American individuals for indefinite service. He learned that Rose had manipulated him, as she was in agreement to his dreadful future outcome. Further, he realized that becoming hypnotized by Rose's mother, without his consent, placed him in a position to be exploited while in an altered susceptible conscious state denying him of his free will. Her being able to take ownership and control over his emotional capacity and physical being under hypnosis primed him for the permanent removal of his global liberties. Under these conditions, Chris was sold to the highest bidder and prepped to undergo a procedure that would merge him and his purchased owner with one another permanently. The successful relocation of Chris's soul to endure the "sunken place" for the remainder of his days would leave Chris with abysmal living conditions and his power and control forever lost with no end to the arrangement.

Within Paz-Fuchs' (2016) description of the attributes that constitute the structure of relationships between captors and enslaved, she elaborated, "it does not suggest that each badge (the seven offered) is necessary nor sufficient for the assertion that slavery exists" (p. 762). However, there is an understanding that the enslaved are "subjected to violence and abuses, to contain them, to control them, to extract their labour against their will and prevent them from leaving their employment", and more importantly, that situations of this nature still occur even today" (David, 2015, p. 151).

Get Out, a complex, multilayered theme film, highlights the onset of a relationship characterized by criteria of slavery and one's fight to remain free. Manipulation, the quest to enslave, envy of another's characteristics, and the relentless desire for freedom all have equal relevance to the making of this film. Frederick Douglass stated, "there is not a man beneath the canopy of heaven, that does not know that slavery is wrong for him" (1852). With that knowledge, once Chris became privy to the scruples of the Armitage family, his will to protect his liberties moved him to engage in what humans have typically done in yesteryear and currently: to persist and effortfully work to become victorious in the pestilent battle for freedom.

Jordan Peele has continued to create films under similar genres of mystery, sci-fi, and horror, creating spaces for Black protagonists to share stories that may highlight racial constructs, yet are not bound by them, such as the subsequent films *Us* (2019) and *Nope* (2022). Rather than marry honesty with comedy, Mr. Peele unifies honesty with horror depicting the chill truth can possess.

Black Panther (2018)

Black Panther was a 200-million-dollar budget film that grossed $1.349 billion at the box office and undeniably created quite a buzz. Being an African American film made it legendary and the highest-earning Black film in history. African American children spoke about the film with one of the most stated comments being, "I like Black Panther and I like seeing myself represented" (https://www.commonsensemedia.org/movie-reviews/black-panther), which allowed for this film to become a key to unlocking the freedom of viewing a cast of nearly all Black people both in power and thriving. Depicting a king, T'Challa/Black Panther (performed by Chadwick Boseman) is a compassionate leader to mankind, who manages conflicts with thoughtfulness and grace. This character shattered the industry's stereotypes of Black men who are frequently viewed within film works as criminals, aggressive, and impoverished. Violence is depicted in a similar manner as per typical superhero films, fighting for what is right and allowing for the hero to conquer. T'Challa/Black Panther's grace exceeds such standards where he not only allows his challengers to live, but encourages them to make the choice to live, understanding power and that the people who follow these men need them.

Acts of betrayal are present within numerous interpersonal exchanges (between T'Challa and his father, between W'Kabi and T'Challa, between Erik and N'Jobu, and between Erik and his family residing in Wakanda). Feelings that arise from being betrayed have "a powerful impact on our lives: They shape our behavior" (Marcatto & Ferrante, 2008, p. 87). We are privy to observing how betrayal and abandonment can combine to create an unwavering desire to be in search of one's beginnings and roots. Similarly it can equally generate desires of retribution consciously and subconsciously by bringing an outside perspective to traditions even when one belongs to the same culture that may significantly differ from the quotidian ways of managing affairs. These changes under the force of authoritarian power can cause harm and trauma where intentions may be positive.

Further and frankly, *Black Panther* was equally beneficial to audiences' travels beyond the stereotypes of individuals in Africa that suggest that Africans are impoverished and in need of rescue. Rather, its desolate landscape is only a front for the world to see to protect the people of Wakanda from being exploited by other countries. Wakanda appears to be a place of infinite abundance, and strength. As the Black Panther's sister, Shuri (performed by Letitia Wright), states, "just because something works doesn't mean that it cannot be improved", a mindset that leads to new inventions and technologies that remain in the imagination for others outside of Wakanda. Viewing such growth and openness to possibilities was empowering and influential encouraging others to equally aspire to great possibility.

And with life events, things change. Within *Black Panther*'s sequel, *Wakanda Forever* (2022), the deaths of the Black Panther/King T'Challa and subsequently Queen Ramonda (performed by Angela Bassett) leave Shuri a grieving sister and daughter. This film highlights the loss of loved ones and the transitions felt from arguably a sister to an only child, from a daughter to an orphan, and from a child to an adult. As a consequence, Shuri begins to contend with who she desires to be and more importantly whom she will emulate: a noble person—like her brother, or a person who will "take care of business" despite the presence of vengeance that motivates her—like her cousin Erik (acted by Michael B. Jordan). Through grief and embodying the Black Panther, Shuri naturally invites an identification with her brother's role as the Black Panther. As safety is a psychological construct that provides security to have space to live freely and excel, being a primitive emotional block for the possibility of forward progression, Shuri harnesses the strength of the Black Panther to first ensure the safety of her people. Once this task is complete, Shuri is finally positioned to be able to use her emotional resources otherwise and grieve the losses she has endured as audiences await what will come next for Wakanda.

If Beale Street Could Talk (2018)

"These are our children and we have to set them free" (Joseph Rivers, performed by Colman Domingo).

Carrying the feeling and holding the reality of being free within one's life is a privileged state. "The power or right to act, speak, or think as one wants without hindrance or restraint" (Oxford English Dictionary, 2024b) is not the life many identify with historically living within America as a person of color. Based on the novel by James Baldwin, *If Beale Street Could Talk* (1974), the interwoven experience of love and being in captivity is a mainstay of the film.

This film depicts the life of Alonzo "Fonny" Hunt (performed by Stephan James) as a man in his early twenties who is incarcerated for the rape of a Latina woman married to a White male, and Tish Rivers (acted by KiKi Layne) who loves Fonny and is pregnant with his child. This film shows the love of this couple that began in their childhood as friends. They find a safety in their love that is sheltered in the history of growing up together in innocence. Their love as emerging adults remains innocent, with a lack of fear for one another, allowing for a tenderness and exploration without boundaries that further cradles them in the feeling of safety. Their bond holds a security and trust that is ever present despite societal bondages that preclude them from having the freedom to find both employment and housing readily and live outside of physical imprisonment.

Whether incarcerated or "free", *If Beale Street Could Talk* illustrates that there are limits and boundaries placed upon one's life as a person of color navigating American soil. Baldwin wrote:

> Fonny had found something that he could do, that he wanted to do, and this saved him from the death that was waiting to overtake the children of our age. Though the death took many forms, though people died early in many different ways, the death itself was very simple and the cause was simple, too: as simple as a plague: the kids had been told that they weren't worth shit and everything they saw around them proved it. They struggled, they struggled, but they fell, like flies, and they congregated on the garbage heaps of their lives, like flies.
>
> (Baldwin, 1974, p. 36)

Within this passage Baldwin takes note of the emotional death that occurs when one lives a life within an environment of the death instinct and in the absence of strong libidinal forces.

Tish, at the young age of nineteen, exhibited insight into the consequences of being enveloped in libidinal forces and secure attachments in her environment. As such, she was attracted to the possibility of living life and building a future with someone. She noted:

> And perhaps I clung to Fonny, perhaps Fonny saved me because he was just about the only boy I knew who wasn't fooling around with the needles or drinking cheap wine or mugging people or holding up stores—and he never got his hair conked: it just stayed nappy. He started working as a short-order cook in a barbecue joint, so he could eat, and he found a basement where he could work on his wood and he was at our house more often than he was at his own house.
>
> (Baldwin, 1974, p. 36)

Within this passage Baldwin takes Fonny to represent survival in a location where survival and thriving are seldom observed, a ray of sunshine in the darkness.

Fonny and Tish's partnership depicts life in love that is prevailing through the various forms of death within their environment and in spite of it. After what they have both been through with one another, neither could claim being innocent in love any longer. They grew up together as children, they became adults together, raised a son, and lived with adult consequences in a society that struggles to see a Black man of color as free. Though, their love appeared protective of one another, even during Fonny's incarceration. Tish's knowledge of his innocence allowed her to remain loving the man she knew him to be. Fonny's ability to have an unwavering "social network of people who understood the unique experience of being wrongfully accused and who did not judge helped him feel able to recover from their experience" (Brooks & Greenberg, 2021, p. 51). The realities of adulthood with the burden of systemic racism sadly sobered Fonny and Tish to love one another in spite of the disappointed pain that ensues in its presence.

Sorry to Bother You (2018)

As children we are taught, by parents and supportive adults, what behaviors are expected to navigate within our society successfully. One aspect of this learning includes adopting societal norms and a moral code that determines when interactions and situations are deemed "right" and what is considered "wrong" for ourselves. As we age, the need for an external figure to inform us of what is right and wrong becomes obsolete, as morality becomes intertwined in the very fabric of who we mature into. Consequently, an individual's compass for right and wrong becomes internalized and even referred to as a "gut feeling", indicative of its deep-rooted placement in one's being. When opportunities arise, we are called to make decisions that reflect one's true self. Even when situations are difficult, we hope that the decisions that are made allow one to sleep soundly at night. However, what happens when one's conscience becomes impaired in being able to make decisions that honor one's true self? Cassius Green (performed by LaKeith Stanfield) in the film *Sorry to Bother You*, written and directed by Boots Riley, illustrates the complications faced when one's conscience is hijacked by external desires for money and success.

In *The Ego and the Id*, Freud (1923) shared his famous tripartite model that included the id that represented one's passions, the ego that described an individual's reason, and the superego representing one's morality. In Freud's account, the conscience was not clearly distinct from the superego (Carveth, 2016). However, in current conceptualizations, the superego and conscience are separate aspects of an individual. On one hand, the conscience is formed in childhood and built on early attachments with caregivers, and "is fueled by attachment and love" (Carveth, 2016, p. 17). The conscience is manifested by the presence of "an inner feeling or voice viewed as acting as a guide to the rightness or wrongness of one's behavior" (Oxford Dictionaries, 2018). On the other hand, the superego involves receiving an internal "judgment and punishment for real or imagined violations of internalized social norms, norms that may sometimes themselves be immoral" and "involves punishment fueled by aggression—mostly turned on the self" (Carveth, 2016, p. 17). As such, we can view that the conscience will provide a loving and supportive perspective of a situation, even at times when poor decisions are made; whereas, the superego will induce self-critical judgment.

Cassius Green is introduced as a young man struggling financially, living with family, who has a strong desire to find employment that will help him feel successful. Upon gaining a position in telemarketing, he finds that he is unsuccessful in sales. Showing frustration, his coworker, Langston (performed by Danny Glover), provides him with a tip that changes the trajectory of his career. He suggests that he uses his "white voice" to speak with customers. After using this tactic, both Cassius's sales and confidence increase significantly and he "finally feels good at something". Because of his superstar performance, he is promoted to become a "Powercaller", one who sells a different set of goods, ones that are promised to earn him significantly greater pay. Cassius learns that being his authentic self must be suppressed to be successful in this environment and the greater the inauthenticity he exhibits, the more successful he becomes. Additionally, with greater success, the less he is able to access his moral compass informing him of what is right and what is wrong for him.

All the while, within scenes at his home and carried into his work cubicle and promoted office, Cassius consults a picture of a man who stands next to a vehicle. This figure, who means a great deal to him, is unidentified and responds directly to Cassius' chosen behaviors. For example, at times, he is found smiling when Cassius views the picture, he is observed frowning and displaying thumbs down when he makes decisions that are questionable, and as being ecstatic when he is proud of his behaviors. This man serves as an externalized image for Cassius, where he consults with the picture to determine the rightness or wrongness of his behaviors. "Regrettably human beings have a tendency to distinguish those who count from those who don't" (Carveth, 2010, p. 115). Upon becoming a Powercaller, Cassius is asked to build his success on the basis of exploiting others and making a conscious decision regarding whose wellbeing counts and whose does not. As he walked down the road of continued success, he was confronted by his friends and fiancée regarding his choices. Cassius struggled to sacrifice his newfound wealth and success; and, only once he was asked to relinquish his humanity to further his career was he able to grasp the gravity and depravity of his circumstance.

"Sometimes our concerns for others puts us in conflict with core elements of our true self" (Carveth, 2016, p. 26). For Cassius, it took a fantastical business proposition to become reacquainted with his true self and awaken him to be concerned for the welfare of others. Carveth (2010) noted that "in order to advance toward a more mature and responsible moral outlook we must" learn to be receptive and answer "to the humane and loving voice of conscience" (p. 108).

So, who is the man in the picture? Might the consultation with this image represent Cassius' conscience? If we were to examine "the two very different types of guilt each [the superego and the conscience] generates: persecutory guilt generated by superego and reparative guilt generated by conscience" (Carveth, 2016, p. 18), then we may rest in that we were introduced to Cassius' true self, false self, and conscience. As the man in the picture displayed his approval and disapproval, never did his role encourage Cassius to torment or punish himself for decisions he made. Rather, this individual in the picture provided an opinion regarding his behaviors and delighted in Cassius' ability to make decisions that helped others while honoring his true self—and, in the process, repair his follies.

At times, making decisions that align with one's true desires can be complicated. When one is posed with an offer and finds oneself at an intersection to do what is considered morally wrong and thereby gain money, success, and other desirables, or to choose the road that requires the individual to do what is considered morally right, yet give up what is desired, for some, the decision may appear quite clear. However, in the event that a regretted decision is made, do not fret. Call upon the services of your conscience to assist and guide you as to what is right with love, acceptance, and the ability to remedy. Give your superego a break from sharing a self-critical view and hope that you can feel your moral compass inside point accurately to excitement and pride by doing what is felt to be right while being your true self in the process.

Queen and Slim (2019)

When two people experience a trauma together, it can create an undeniable bond. Experiencing with another the intensities of emotions that surface in the face of crisis can create a feeling that the other is the only person in the world who can understand what is happening and the feelings experienced. Survival of the crisis becomes paramount and causes one to bond with the individual who shares the space of the trauma. As a result, the experience of trauma can isolate the victims and limits who is relatable and able to provide help. Within the film *Queen and Slim*, these two characters encounter one evening together that changes the course of their lives creating a passionate intimacy between the pair

Queen (performed by Jodie Turner Smith) is introduced as a criminal defense attorney upon her first date with Slim (acted by Daniel Kaluuya), a grocery store clerk. With a slow beginning for the two, they ultimately enjoy their evening becoming acquainted with one another until they are pulled over by the police for swerving the vehicle. The police officer Reed approaches the car in a hostile manner which concludes with him threatening to shoot Slim. Out of self-defense, Slim obtains the officer's weapon, shoots, and mistakenly kills him. Queen educates Slim regarding the realities of his defense, indicating that these behaviors will result in him being imprisoned, where he will become property of the state. Offering this picture of his future, she suggests that the two of them escape the law and become fugitives. News alerts regarding these events are broadcast nationwide, leading to protests within the African American community supporting freeing Queen and Slim. Their presence is understood as an active Bonnie and Clyde tale. Individuals in the African American community support them, promising that they can offer a safe shelter, albeit temporarily, along their journey.

In reality, there are only a few who can state that they have undergone an experience similar to that of Queen and Slim. The uniqueness of the events that take place positions them in a space where individuals can easily empathize deeply with them. Though, no one but the two of them could understand fully the distress, fear, sadness, hope coupled with hopelessness, and intimacy between the two that arose from such an incident and the choices that followed thereafter. Such intense

90 Unchained... Freedom (2010–2019)

intimacy is built upon a trust that developed quickly and intensely based upon the crisis and from a desire for survival. With an understanding that they both have everything to lose, they realize that they are the only two individuals who possess the same quality of safety with the same level of determination of achieving it. Consequently, they become one another's life force lending hope to each other when needed and sharing in hope when lucky.

Legacy Films

12 Years a Slave (2012)

When one is free, it is a condition and state of mind that can be taken for granted. Being present and in the here and now is many times hailed as an emotional accomplishment that assists in psychological wellbeing. However, there are times that being present in one's circumstance causes one to lack awareness of others' lived experiences, especially when the lived experience is one that is rooted in injustice, suffering, and trauma. Trauma is a phenomenon that lends itself to both emotional and cognitive disorganization:

> Trauma also overwhelms and defeats our capacity to organise it: facing real acts of massive aggression, our psychological abilities are rendered ineffective. Massive aggression's pervasive, deconstructive impact on the cultural and psychological assumptions governing our lives often results in a cognitive and affective paralysis, from whose vantage point we can only relate to the events as if they had not happened. At times this extends as far as denial of their historical veracity.
>
> (Laub & Auerhahn, 1993, p. 287).

As a result, "we look to victims of trauma to tell us about it. Narrative is often considered to be the 'solution to... the problem of how to translate *knowing* into *telling*, the problem of fashioning human experience into a form assimilable to structures of meaning' and comprehensible to others" (White, 1980, p. 5; emphases in the original). Depending upon the lived traumatic experiences of others to conceive of the horrors that existed within antebellum America is where *12 Years a Slave* was born. Solomon Northup (performed by Chiwetel Ejiofor) created a written document of his experience of being abducted and sold into slavery as a free man residing in upstate New York. *12 Years a Slave* provides a cinematic depiction of his written account of living in the United States as an enslaved man.

At the onset of this film, the audience is introduced to Solomon Northup as a talented, sought-after violinist, a loving husband, and a dedicated father to his two children. As a gentleman, he is well groomed in three piece suits and fashions accompanying hats that show his well-established financial standing. The manner in which he converses with his White peers, whom he considers his friends, illustrates his educational foundation is sound and he traverses through life as a man that appears untouched by slavery that occurs in states below him. Born free in 1807 by his free mother of color and to a father freed from slavery, Solomon Northup's exposure to the aggression of what slavery produced is unknown in this film. Thus, his response to individuals who may have desired his assistance in securing freedom may have gone unnoticed as an unidentifiable occurrence based upon his lack of knowing what that type of interaction would entail. For instance, while he patronized a local store for provisions, he spoke with his friend and heard the door of the store open. When he offered an inquiring look, he found an African American man who appeared intrigued by him. Before Mr. Northup was able to address the man, a White man hurried into the store and forgave the Black man for interrupting. Mr. Northup appeared unaffected, even dismissive of the encounter and continued with his exchange with his friend. It is unclear who the man was and no information was provided regarding the man's social status. Though, the man appeared desperate to make Mr. Northup's acquaintance to discover more about him. Might this man have been a man in captivity desiring to find a person who could facilitate his freedom? Yet, at this time, Mr. Northup is unknowing of the man and his circumstance and chooses to remain so by accepting the forgiveness of the White man. In this early moment in the film, Mr. Northup is a person who lives in the world as one who is knowing yet primarily unknowing of the trauma of other African Americans which affords him the life of fulfillment that he experiences.

> Much of knowing is dependent on language—not only our knowing trauma through hearing the victims' language, but the ability of victims to grasp and re-call their experiences through the process of formulating them in language. Be-cause of the radical break between trauma and culture, victims often cannot find categories of thought or words for their experience. That is, since neither culture nor experience provide structures for formulating acts of massive aggression, survivors cannot articulate trauma, even to themselves. Furthermore, knowing, in the sense of articulation, analysis, elaboration, and reformulation, requires the preservation of a detached sensibility, which is destroyed in situations of horror.
>
> (Laub & Auerhahn, 1993, p. 288)

Mr. Northup's refined language abilities afford a salient account of his twelve years providing a vivid narrative of life enslaved. Though his language abilities while in bondage suggested to others that his previous life before they encountered him was one of freedoms, individuals who forced labor from him allowed themselves to be held in a position of unknowing, ignoring the observable fact that this language and the experiences he articulated were suggestive of a free man. Instead, individuals appreciated his innovative contributions and "rewarded" him (i.e. by purchasing him a violin) that ultimately further exploited him when individuals demanded him to play in the middle of the night for entertainment rather than obtain a sound sleep after a long day of laboring in the cotton fields.

Once captured, attempts were made to strip Mr. Northup from his previous identity as a free man. Indoctrinating him into the belief that he is a slave with a specific past through verbal, emotional, and physical assaults created an environment that made it impossible for him to continue living in the state of unknowing the pains of slavery. As he begins to experience the trauma of the institution first-hand, Mr. Northup is forced to shift his position and be in a state of all-knowing of what possibly awaits him in order to maintain his life in the face of threats upon it, while at the same time, he is asked to unknow his history. This fluctuation of knowing and unknowing is desired by all, both the slaves and those who hold them in captivity. For instance, Mistress Ford (acted by Liza J. Bennett) suggests to Eliza (performed by Adepero Oduye), when observing her wail in grief once her children are sold to others in slavery and the family is separated, that after a good meal and rest she will forget her children existed. The fantasy that food and sleep will erase one's history of one's loved ones supports the well-entrenched defenses that render one's thought processes in traumatic situations as reality bending. Mistress Ford's fantasy also reveals that she too in this environment of unsafety for those around her must equally live in a state of unknowing and knowing, witnessing the inhumane treatment of the African Americans working on her plantation and holding a state of unknowing that they are human, with human desires and emotions who withstand persistent, vicious aggressions. For those who were unable to unknow, such as Eliza who loudly grieved her lost children, poor futures awaited. Lack of tolerance of active grief caused Mr. Northup to begin to lack patience and reveal his frustration with her lack of resilience and attempt to make it through the situation. Yet, dissimilarly, Mr. Northup had a life of freedom, literacy, and the will to return to his life of freedom. As some of his enslaved peers were "born and raised slaves", the hopelessness that accompanied their situation further fueled the abysmal reality of their existence. Being free was entirely an unknown reality leaving one to only know what one had always had.

> We all hover at different distances between knowing and not knowing about trauma, caught between the compulsion to complete the process of knowing and the inability or fear of doing so. It is the nature of trauma to elude our knowledge, because of both defence and deficit. The knowledge of trauma is fiercely defended against, for it can be a momentous, threatening, cognitive and affective task, involving an unjaundiced appraisal of events and our own injuries, failures, conflicts and losses.
>
> (Laub & Auerhahn, 1993, p. 287)

It is understandable that in living a life of one's own it is difficult to be attuned to the lives of others. Being preoccupied with one's concerns can cause one to be myopic and lack awareness and interest in attending to the sufferings of others. This concept is charged for contemplation within the film *Boys N the Hood* (1991) when Ice Cube's character states that individuals either may be unaware or do not care about the tragedies that occur in the hood. Similar sentiments are mentioned in the film *The Great Debaters* (2007) when Henry Lowe confronts his fellow debater, James Farmer, Jr., regarding the feelings had once witnessing a lynching.

It was also admitted within the film *Till* (2022), which will be discussed further in the following chapter. Though it may be seductive to lean into protecting ourselves from our intense "feelings of rage, cynicism, shame, and fear by not knowing them consciously" (Laub & Auerhahn, 1993, p. 288), these defenses may be best evoked temporarily in the service of allowing one to generate the emotional fortitude to survive traumatic experiences with the intention of returning to safety and remain knowing for the need to recover and possibly become a healing force in helping to resolve circumstances of human suffering.

Selma (2014)

Living an existence of freedom in America for an African American individual has historically been one of challenge. Though African American men were legally granted the right to vote in America, in 1865–1866, "most Southern state legislatures enacted restrictive laws known as Black codes, which strictly governed Black citizens' behaviors and denied them suffrage and other rights" (Pruitt, 2021). Contributing to elections to have one's voice heard is a privilege recognized within the African American community. Thus, the right to and the execution of a vote are not taken lightly. When voter suppression was enacted in Selma, Alabama, activists led by the Reverend Dr. Martin Luther King, Jr. took to the Edmund Pettus Bridge to demonstrate, by peaceful protest, the support the African American community had to obtain voter registration.

Selma is a film that showcases the events that occurred in Selma for state law to accept African Americans' right to vote. Civil and police brutality, protests, lynchings, and tear gas were all a part of the experience for those who risked their lives to achieve the ease of gaining registration to vote. And though this part of history is our history, we continue to witness its residue in voter-suppressive behaviors in the present day. It is only with continued activism by dedicated activists that African Americans are able to access the voting polls safely. When drawn to such a film, individuals tend to desire to learn regarding the history and understand where we are today and how we arrived to our present. Yet, there are additional aspects of the film that may be overlooked and placed as less pivotal due to the compelling energy and accomplishments of our civil rights leaders in the film. Though, Paul Webb (screenwriter) and Ava DuVernay (director) included in this film the relationships that Dr. Martin Luther King established and maintained. This aspect of the film depicts that Selma was as a community-fueled event spearheaded by the leadership of Dr. Martin Luther King, Jr. and the sacrifices and distress of many. As Dr. Martin Luther King, Jr. interfaced with numerous individuals that influenced his ability to galvanize the African American community to protest while individuals were viciously awaiting to aggress, he relied upon the consultation of politicians, colleagues, his wife, and his Lord, all of whom made essential contributions to his civic efforts.

Throughout the course of the film Dr. Martin Luther King, Jr.'s position in relation to political heads is clear. His meetings with the President of the United

States, Lyndon B. Johnson, demonstrate that Dr. King's efforts have been substantial to have the constant ear of the President. And, indeed, his efforts led to great change before the protests in Selma occurred, earning him the Nobel Peace Prize in 1964. His conversations with the President in an effort to consult on civil rights issues were carefully crafted. Relying upon the use of the media and news outlets, Dr. Martin Luther King, Jr. was successfully able to move the needle forward to ensure voter registration rights were enforced.

And an army from the African American community was needed for the planned success. Consultation, negotiation, and decision making were implemented with like-minded colleagues to create a united front. Although final decisions regarding how protests proceeded were left to the determination of Dr. Martin Luther King, Jr. in the film, he relied upon his colleagues to share their understanding of the circumstances, to place priority on the issues, assist to devise logistics around the march in Selma, and support the energies of others to engage. Despite his having the ability to be in the Oval Office of the White House to speak with the President, ultimately community connections were the driving force for change.

Further, being the wife of a civil rights leader bears its burdens. In true partnership, Dr. Martin Luther King, Jr. consulted with his wife, Coretta Scott King, regarding the state of affairs. Within the film it appears that many times he discussed ways for his wife to remain abreast of the progression of the movement. Consequently, when he was incarcerated, she became responsible for discussions with Malcolm X in the absence of her husband's knowledge initially to keep up the momentum while he was detained. The film also depicted that discussions with his wife allowed for conversations to leave the logistical realm and provided him opportunities to contemplate the existential impact of being an activist. His home with her was a place to be able to communicate his fears and for her to communicate hers within the boundaries of respecting the gravity of the topics and in the absence of creating jokes about the true dangers they faced. The reality was that within protests lives were struck down by the blunt force of police officers' clubs and in the safety of their home harassing threats were received regarding how death would come upon him and his family. Lives of activists would be lost within marches. It is in the space he had with his wife that he was able to have a moment to be quiet, listen, and sit with the feelings that he and his wife felt mutually.

Lastly, Dr. Martin Luther King, Jr. consulted his Lord. As a Baptist minister, the locations in which he spoke to the community frequently occurred at the pulpit, a familiar place for the Reverend Dr. Martin Luther King, Jr. When required, he kneeled and prayed regarding whether progressing with a march would be safe and in the group's best interest. The film illustrates that the Lord dictated his steps and would stop a march from progressing when necessary. This experience was observed when demonstrators wondered what was happening when they arrived to the Edmund Pettus Bridge, faced police officers, and turned around in silence. At that time, falling to his knees to pray, he acquiesced to what was communicated to him to protect himself and others from what was known to be a dangerous territory.

The Reverend Dr. Martin Luther King relied upon a community of like-minded brave citizens who desired a fair way of navigating America. In doing so, these activists endured conflicts, hardships, and grief in the service of protesting when civil rights were violated. These members of the community served as protective factors for Dr. Martin Luther King, Jr., engaging him in confronting conversations and comforting him by singing to him in the middle of the night to place his soul at ease. There are only a few who can dedicate their lives to the causes of others. When a sole person can do so, they require an inner fortitude to resist against the conflicts that await. Possessing protective factors can act as an essential aspect of self-care that allows one to persevere for the service of all.

Hidden Figures (2016)

Please find upon pages 113–132 in *Best Psychology in Film* (Marshall Woods, 2018).

Detroit (2017)

On July 23rd, 1967 in Detroit a five-day series of riots occurred within predominately African American neighborhoods. Looting, burning of buildings, and police brutality were present. Due to the destructiveness, the National Guard and Army troops were solicited to dismantle protests. Within these five days, an incident at the Algiers Motel began on July 25th and ended on July 26th involving ten African American teenage and emerging adult males and two White female emerging adults when officials began to search the premises for a possible sniper. The result of this search included the deaths of three Black teenagers (Carl Cooper, age 19; Aubrey Pollard, age 19; and Fred Temple, age 18) by gunshot and all other parties being severely wounded. Being held in captivity can shift an individual's thoughts and feelings so greatly that the individual and others may feel that though they have survived they are now unrecognizable. Dreams once possessed may be perceived differently, leaving one to reconsider who remains as a result of the trauma experienced. For some, a part of oneself dies despite surviving what can be considered a hostage situation of torture.

According to the Oxford English Dictionary (2024a), "the condition of being imprisoned or confined" defines whether an individual experiences captivity. When one is in captivity an individual may also be a hostage, one that is "seized or held as security for the fulfillment of a condition" (Oxford English Dictionary, 2024c). The individuals in the Algiers Motel, confined in the motel with police officials, were informed that they were being held to fulfill the condition of locating a person believed to have a firearm. For some, this may be a point of debate. Is it the police's duty to confine individuals who are a threat to society? Within this incident, the police's search for a firearm was unsuccessful. The individuals held shared that there were no weapons on the premises. Despite this and their later pleas, they remained in captivity as hostages waiting for a firearm that would never materialize

96 Unchained... Freedom (2010–2019)

to satisfy the officials. "In situations of captivity the perpetrator becomes the most powerful person in the life of the victim" (Herman, 1992, p. 75), whereas in this incident, this combination of events resulted in what the Oxford English Dictionary would describe as torture (2024d): "the action or practice of inflicting severe pain on someone as a punishment or to force them to do or say something, or for the pleasure of the person inflicting the pain".

Larry (performed by Algee Smith) in the film *Detroit* illustrates this interpersonal dynamic after being victimized within the Algiers Motel with his musical group's valet by his side. An aspiring vocal artist and the lead singer of the budding group, The Dramatics, Larry was enthusiastic, hopeful, and believed in his bright future. He was dedicated to his craft and had confidence that his dream of being a singer would become reality. However, once held against his will in the motel by police officials and holding the knowledge that multiple individuals were killed including his valet and friend, Fred (acted by Jacob Latimore), Larry's ability to engage, display hope, and believe in his future shifted dramatically. The experience of that evening and morning impacted him so greatly that when his dream could be actualized in a studio with individuals wanting to sign the group thereafter, he was unable to desire performing in the way he had before the incident. Once freed from that evening, one could question whether he was truly free immediately after the event; how could he be? This experience that concluded in the deaths of many, including his friend, ultimately killed the dream he had for himself.

Not all was lost in the face of such events. Grieving and facing the realities of needing work, Larry finds a way to transform his musical talents into serving as a choir director. Once an individual has experienced a trauma, the recovery process can be a time of rebirth. Acknowledging that one can never return to the person they once were prior to the trauma creates an opportunity to recreate, and integrate one's past self, the grief, and loss to reclaim feeling remotely whole again.

Marshall (2017)

> "We will only attain freedom if we learn to appreciate what is different and muster the courage to discover what is fundamentally the same."
>
> (Thurgood Marshall, 1992).

Fighting for freedom is not a novel experience. For centuries wars have been fought to gain freedoms for respective groups of citizens. African Americans have fought for freedom for centuries upon this soil for varying reasons. Freedom to possess one's body as their own, the fight to be considered human, and the fight to vote freely have all been battles in which African Americans have seen combat. Thurgood Marshall for whom the film *Marshall* is named depicts an attorney, whom we know later becomes a Justice of the Supreme Court, who represents in his early career African Americans who were falsely accused of a crime. Working for The National Association for the Advancement of Colored People (NAACP)

Legal Defense Fund as their lead attorney, Mr. Marshall had the supports of an organization to represent individuals in legal distress readily.

Thurgood Marshall was prolific in his efforts and achievements. "He was the one black lawyer in this country in the modern pre-Civil Rights era who always had the big picture in mind," says Haygood in Boissoneault, (2017). Each legal case he engaged, if resolved with a favorable judgment, had the potential not only to save the defendant's life, both literally and figuratively, but to move the needle for future cases for African Americans. The film captures the importance of a specific legal case that fosters Mr. Marshall to cultivate the legal talents of a co-counsel, Sam Friedman, which led to a friendship being created. Although details of the case coupled by Marshall and Friedman's budding friendship are largely what the film attends to, what can become minimized in this inspiring film are the sacrifices of time, physical integrity, and love that individuals make to live a freedom fighter's life.

Mr. Marshall travels from city to city to represent individuals in legal need. "He would file voting rights cases, employment rights cases, criminal justice cases, housing discrimination cases, and all of these victories became the blueprint for the 1964 Civil Rights Bill and the 1965 Voting Rights Act" (Haygood in Boissoneault, 2017). Within the film, Marshall concludes a case only to begin a case in Connecticut that the audience is able to follow from beginning to end. However, due to demand, Mr. Marshall cannot meet the audience at the trial's conclusion, as he is called away to a Southern state to represent another client in need leaving all parties, including the audience, behind to learn the verdict. Over a landline where words are nearly incomprehensible, Marshall hears from his friend Sam that his efforts have led to a "not guilty" verdict. Overjoyed, he is placed at ease and able to begin his next case with confidence. His time, no longer his own, is used to fight for the lives of others.

In his important role Mr. Marshall's life had a great deal of hustle and bustle. Spending time in his home with his wife was cherished time, taken in between cases and travels. Life events that occurred at home were communicated when he was miles away, where he held the desire to be close and near. For example, Mr. Marshall's wife miscarries a child, where there is a range of feelings exhibited with the news. Verbally articulated is his disappointment at being away, "I should be there", yet the reality including his position limits his ability to be present, even in the worst times for him and his loved one.

Further, Thurgood Marshall's role, similar to most civil rights activists, placed him in a position of being physically assaulted by the cruelty of hate in others. When individuals engaged in civil activism and demonstrated a willingness to be altruistic to those who faced discrimination and systemic racism, others threatened and angrily demonstrated their emotions by physically acting out and aggressing upon courageous civic leaders. Regardless of what and whom he faced, Mr. Marshall represented his commitment to civil rights and the freedom of the African American people wrongly accused, demonstrating both competence and power. In turn, these characteristics provoked those with aggression towards racial issues to enact their hate towards him and those around him. As Mr. Marshall is physically assaulted in a public location, his friend Sam, a White American, is also physically attacked for his professional association with Mr. Marshall.

It is not atypical that employment can cause compromises in a person's life. Time spent at work, being away from family, the stressors, and the demands can be emotionally burdensome. For those civil rights activists working tirelessly on behalf of individuals in dire circumstances, the sacrifices might surpass typical limits. The ordinary desire to walk away and take back their time is paused. The availability to be with loved ones, and the ability to gain assurance of their physical integrity are shelved for their values—to push forward for mankind. The extraordinary heard cries of others, as whimpering as they may be—individuals such as these brave activists find space to comfort others and fight for their opportunity to live.

6

Awaiting with Baited Breath (2020 and Beyond)

In 2020, the world changed. Diligently, the media documented medical professionals' temporarily scared faces due to chronic mask-wearing. Hospitals were featured being overwhelmed by patients struggling to breathe, on ventilators, or worse, being wheeled out to the street in bags to be added to freezers housing additional corpses that lost the battle with Covid-19. As individuals sheltered in place, media consumption increased significantly not only as a form of entertainment, but as a way to manage anxieties and utilize time spent primarily indoors. According to Shapiro (2020), the increase in home streaming films and media was reflected in stock increases that were the highest since 2018 for companies like Netflix, and a 49% increase in usage across three months (January–March 2020, the first months of "shelter in place" orders provided by states) for Roku (Shapiro, 2020). What was viewed were persons' favorite films, and completed media that were scheduled for a 2020 release. Due to the success of streaming platforms, major media outlets that lacked a robust streaming platform galvanized energies towards creating one to meet their consumers' hunger and to capitalize on the profits available at the time. In the meantime, movie theaters were vacant and many succumbed to the economic downward shift some in-person industries experienced and closed their doors permanently.

Through this time, media makers continued to work. Covid-19 protocols to allow production teams to continue to create began to be built. Vaccines for Covid-19 became available, making safer environments for people for whom, though they could contract Covid-19, the implications may not have been as dire. And when situations finally felt safe medically, economically individuals in the industry struggled. Then in 2023, the Writers Guild of America's strike began, halting productions for a second time in the decade. Today, mere days into 2024, the release of productions has been limited in a manner that is reminiscent of days past for African American artists but for reasons most could not have predicted would occur in succession.

And yet, there has been an abundance of indie films that were produced within this time, and compelling studio films within this decade that provided a promising foundation for future African American film work. The following below are a few of such films. With that stated, it is important to also note the contribution streaming platforms made to the production of films that were exclusive for their platforms. Many of these films, though not highlighted directly within this text, are equally meaningful in terms of the impact they have had within the African American community. When these films are examined, their applicability to the way we understand relations, ourselves, and the world is enhanced.

Da 5 Bloods (2020)

Within many cultures death is an expected part of living while being an emotionally challenging time in one's life. In response, ceremonies are arranged that allow the loss of a loved one to be grieved in a contained, predictable way. These events provide the opportunity to honor the lost person and honor the impact they have had on others' lives. However, there are circumstances when having the opportunity to say goodbye is compromised and made impossible. War can pose as an obstacle that does not offer one's loved ones the opportunity to say goodbye in a way one would prefer.

In times of war, saying goodbye to one's losses can be an overwhelming task. There may be a great deal of losses had. The loss of one's personal personality, one's typical characteristics, physical amputations, the understanding of self, losing comrades, and at times one's emotional functioning are present in mind for our veterans. When war ends, despite how much can be recovered, many times what is discovered is that everyone is forever changed and an internal war continues to ensue. For Paul (acted by Delroy Lindo), Otis (depicted by Clarke Peters), Melvin (acted by Isiah Whitlock, Jr.), and Eddie (performed by Norm Lewis), these comrades returned after decades to recover what was left behind from the Vietnam War: the body of their fallen comrade and millions' worth in gold bars. What was exposed and recovered during this trip was more than what appeared to be known at the onset of the journey.

When the men arrived, they recounted experiences and caught up regarding their lives. During these initial scenes, Eddie presented as a friend who was of financial means, insisting that he placed everyone's stay at the hotel on his American Express card. Paul appears skeptical to individuals, was easily agitated, and uninhibited in sharing his skepticism with others. Otis continued to have contacts in Vietnam allowing him to take the lead on managing the logistics of how to ship the found gold to the United States once recovered. Melvin offered the friends a stable opinion and attempted to quell upsets that the group experienced. These early scenes are a prelude to the dynamics seen throughout the film. Otis learning that he has an adult daughter with his former lover, the group learning that Eddie is financially unsound, and Paul's experiences of a poor interpersonal relationship with his son David (acted by Jonathan Majors) and sufferings from severe symptoms of post-traumatic stress disorder (PTSD) are psychologically forward concepts offered at the onset of the film. What is learned is that these men's deployment exposed them to combat experiences (i.e. exposures to receiving enemy fire, and witnessing the death of a member of their unit) that would make it likely to have symptoms of PTSD as Paul demonstrated (Henschel & McDevitt-Murphy, 2016).

At its conclusion, this film highlights that returning to the site of war has the potential to foster both external and internal closure. Finding their fallen comrade's skeleton buried where they placed him, forgiving oneself for mistakes that have shaped their lives, and locating the gold fostered opportunities for final goodbyes to be paid and closure to a chapter of these men's lives to be granted. This challenging journey depicted in this film highlights how a fertile ground for recovery also is laden with emotional harshness. The parallel this film makes demonstrates that most recoveries include specific ingredients. Particularly, additional loss may be suffered leaving one's state of denial to address challenges as needed. Healthy interpersonal relationships that are characterized by vulnerability and compromise suggest that even when a war has concluded and closures may have been achieved, one's internal war may persist until one gently interweaves healing as a conscious process.

The Photograph (2020)

Within psychodynamic theory, it is understood that one's early childhood shapes the experiences of one's adult life. Feelings had, decisions made, and actions that are taken can many times be traced back to the root of how one presents today. One's family can serve as the soil that grounds a person. It is hoped that the soil in which one is planted is nutrient rich and abundant allowing for plants to blossom and bear a fruitful life. However, for some, the soil lacks richness in some areas, allowing some plants to prosper while others are left wanting—and at worst, to wither. Within the film *The Photograph*, Mae (performed by Issa Rae) experiences a conflictual relationship with her mother, Christina Eames (depicted by Chanté Adams), as she works through the grief of her mother's death.

Mae presents as an intelligent creative employed as an Assistant Director of an art gallery in Queens, New York. Learning that her mother was a photographer, it is understood that Mae bears similar artistic talents and skill to her. Mae's mother becomes of interest to a reporter, Michael (performed by LaKeith Stanfield), while he writes a story of a man in New Orleans who once was in love with her. When he seeks to see her mother's photographs, there is a connection that Mae has to him. Naturally, when he attends the art gallery's film screening and she sees him at the end of the evening, they have their first date. Upon their date, Mae vulnerably, in an admission that appears to hold little consequence, discloses that she does not know who she is. In fact, later when speaking with the man who fathered her about her relationship with her mother, Louis Morton (acted by Courtney B. Vance), she describes the many ways that she does not wish to identify with her mother. Rather, she offers ways in which the soil her mother had her rooted in as a child was deficient leaving her emotionally longing. As a result, not only does she not wish to be like her mother in these ways, she fears she already exhibits similarities to her mother—in particular, within the area of being capable of loving another.

When Mae begins to pursue continuing to get to know Michael and learns that he may relocate to London for work, she struggles to communicate her authentic feelings to him. She desires him to remain in New York and to observe what buds the relationship may flower, yet suggests the opposite, sharing a bleak forecast for what the relationship would hold. Struggling to understand herself is reflected in her difficulty in being able to know and accept her authentic feelings towards Michael, and to articulate them to him when he explicitly asks what she desires from the relationship. Mae admits that within that moment with Michael, she is unable to share her true feelings due to her lack of feeling worthy of asking him to rearrange his employment and life for the possibility of what their relationship could be with time. This experience between Mae and Michael becomes a beautifully illustrated reenactment as defined as "an earlier experience, relationship or feeling state" (Howell, 2020, p. 68), as Mae places herself in a relational dynamic where her emotional needs go unmet and neglected, reflecting a similar dynamic she experienced as a child with her mother. Reenactments, unconscious repetitions of relational dynamics, tend to occur when there is a lack of examination of a past relational experience and acknowledgement of the significant impact that the dynamic has had upon one's life. Rather than being able to move forward, one attempts to rework the conflict in new relationships until mastered. The individual in the reenactment has greater control of experiencing the feeling than in the past, as their behavior(s) invite the reenactment to occur. For example, Mae found herself with unmet emotional needs due to her mother's challenges with displaying love to others and placed her energies into her work. Mae as a young child had no control over this experience; as her mother acted, and Mae experienced the feelings that surfaced as a result. Yet, with Michael, Mae actively withholds her true feelings (aligning with her mother), which ultimately places her in the similar space of not being able to get her emotional needs met by the other individual, allowing her to feel emotionally wanting again and in similar ways to what she felt when she was a child with her mother.

To exit a reenactment takes significant introspective examination and a conscious understanding of the impact the dynamic has had upon one's lived experience. Mae begins to learn more about her mother and herself by a letter that her mother leaves to her to read once she has died. She is provided information regarding the history of the soil in which she was planted by her mother and gains a better understanding of why the soil was both rich and abundant while being deficient and barren concurrently. Further, upon this journey, Mae receives nutrients from a surprising place which fosters her ability to trust that she can love vulnerably and is better able to allow herself to fulfill her emotional needs and bloom in the possibility of love.

The Woman King (2022)

In the nuances of every film there are numerous psychological dynamics that prompt one to engage in the characters and the themes present. *The Woman King* is similar as it contains a variety of psychological underpinnings able to be considered.

Specifically, individuals and formed groups holding a shared commitment was a heartbeat theme throughout the film.

Nanisca (performed by Viola Davis) holds the most striking and obvious commitments shown. As a general, she is center stage in demonstrating a commitment to the service she provides to the king. She is engaged politically holding in mind social constructs, informing him of alternative ways to secure the financial survival of their tribe while ensuring that all of the women warriors are equally committed to protecting the throne. In her role she demonstrates commitment to the integrity of Africa's promise to prosper outside of the transatlantic slave trade, swimming vigorously upstream to ensure that it is clear to the king that they are abundant in natural resources and do not have to sell their people. This responsibility and commitment is not without sacrifice. She explains that there is no ability to have intimacies with a man, a loving relationship with a paramour, and one in this position will also shun the option of having children. Nanisca's commitment is branded upon her scarred body and is worn in a manner that adorns her. As she shows her battle marks to Nawi (acted by Thuso Mbedu) there is not pride or shame present, but there in these scars lies the history of a warrior.

The prohibition of the Agojie women to have a male intimate partnership and build a family to demonstrate one's commitment to the role of a warrior is a substantial ask. Such a requirement reinforces the stereotype held currently and in America that women are "less than fully committed to labor force activities, in large measure because of their traditional responsibilities to family and home" (Moen & Smith, 1986, p. 450). The authors noted, "It is fair to say that women as well as men are increasingly making an emotional investment in their jobs and many find employment an important source of identity", yet "regardless to their marital status, women are perceived not primarily as workers but as family members" (p. 451). In an effort for there to be a lack of confusion to the commitment and loyalty these women dedicated to protecting the throne of the king, the choice is made at the onset of training, being transparent that no space is made to hold both roles. Moen and Smith's (1986) research revealed there is variability in the work commitment possessed by women based upon the roles they balance. Specifically, they found younger women who have not yet begun to build a family and have been in the workforce for at minimum five years are more likely to have a greater commitment to their employment. Further, "for young women without family obligations we find a high level of congruence between psychological commitment and patterns of employment behavior. We also see higher levels of commitment among the non-married than married women" (p. 470), though women with children can equally be committed to their employment once married and raising children, but the authors noted that "other considerations beyond psychological investment may be operating to keep them in the labor force" (p. 470) such as financial obligations. Thus, though some women made a sacrifice to commit completely to warrior life as depicted in the film, it was perhaps believed that having relationships such as intimate male partnership and having children would compete with their allegiance to the throne.

The film depicts near the onset a neophyte group of women who are in training, seeking to earn the status and privilege of becoming Agojie warriors. The complexity of Nawi's will, that is described as arrogant, is a strong addition to this film. Specifically, as a young woman, she is introduced with the obligation that she must take a husband. Her father frequently introduces her to men whom she does not wish to marry. Consequently, she is viewed as an obstinate child and is physically assaulted as a result of her commitment to her freedom. Due to her opposition, when her care is given to the king by her father, she finds women whom she desires to emulate and her commitment shifts to becoming a warrior. Being misunderstood as a woman who has had an "easy life", her dedication to building her skills to serve the king is both challenged and confronted. These interactions appear to be accepted by her as a catalyst to demonstrate her budding techniques in an explosive way. With conviction she shows persistence, fortitude, and her power. Regardless of the number of trials she faces, she excels beyond the performance of her peers to prove that she is fit for the life of an Agojie.

This feel-strong, feel-good film allows audiences to leave empowered by the sisterhood of the Agojie warriors, having imbibed pride regarding the influence of women, and feeling recognized for our strength. Included in the initial pages of this book, stereotypes of Black women represented on the silver screen were explored. *The Woman King*, being inspired by true events, is a film refreshingly absent of these roles that tend to plague female characters within film. Because this film depicts the life of individuals during the transatlantic slave trade on African soil, it is questionable whether the classic stereotypes of women in film are truly applicable. These tropes of African American women tend to illustrate life once it began on American soil. Additionally, the time period in which this film is set, 1823, may also shepherd female characters outside of these constraining roles.

To showcase a narrative that surfaces the topic of when purchasing Africans for the slave trade became an unacceptable enterprise in Africa, and a king's support for locating natural resources to trade as an alternative was a brave endeavor. Consequently, female stereotypes were not the most compelling cause for critics' critiques. Particularly, the minimization of the presence and quality of behaviors that ensued from slavery in Dahomey was an area that is "equal parts disturbing and important" as noted by Andy (2023). As psychological accuracy is suggested to be important for audiences' awareness and knowledge, such historical accuracies are equally paramount. Andy (2023) continued that "the producers and creators of *The Woman King* had to know that they were stepping into a landmine with the creation of a film featuring such a sensitive topic". It is hypothesized that this film lost an opportunity to depict "the fascinating realities of one of the most tragic atrocities in human history in a respectful and honest manner" (Andy, 2023), cementing the importance and impact accuracy in films has upon audiences in a global way.

American Fiction (2023)

American Fiction is rich with many psychological concepts that remain constantly available to follow throughout the duration of the film. Contending with family dynamics that range from experiencing the sourness and pain of family members, to disappointments and sibling and parent–child relationships while caring for an elderly parent, were topics of intrapsychic and interpersonal connection. Career disenchantment, engaging in the onset of a romantic relationship, and being the child of suicide were also aspects of the human experience that were present for exploration. Though, the most ever-present dynamics were laid in the character of Thelonious "Monk" Ellison (acted by Jeffrey Wright).

As a writer of classical literature, Monk finds himself riddled with conflictual feelings that appear flamed in a crucible of frustration by America seeking and rewarding Black stories with stereotypical characters. Themes he noticed in these works tended to include violence, parent–child conflict, absent fathers, and untimely pregnancies. His response to audiences' favorable taking to such artwork cloaked him with disgust that left in its wake an individual who desired to retreat due to his inability to feel able to relate to, or even tolerate, others. Insightfully, Monk was aware of his challenge connecting, as many experienced him as both withdrawn and disgruntled. Despite his insight, he was unable to alter his presentation to be better equipped to connect with others and for others to be better able to engage with him.

Monk's brother and sister are introduced professionally as physicians. Monk being a doctor of philosophy considered himself the sibling who was different. Because he continued to pursue literature and became a professor, his pensive nature would possibly be understandable, even an asset in his career field as a writer and as an academic. Once he returns home, he learned that both his siblings have recently finalized their divorces and have experienced a loss. He finds his sister being the primary caregiver of their mother and his brother beginning to embrace his life as a gay man. Monk's disconnection to his family is overtly noted by both his siblings. He is known for lacking value in cultivating reciprocal intimate relations and pushing others away. However, Monk very much desires to be loved, yet craved to receive such admiration through being a beloved and successful author rather than from the intimacies that relationships could offer. Yet, due to his uncompromising rigidity and judgment that others' work was mediocre at best, his standards sheltered him to remain removed in elitist expectations that most would never meet.

In contrast, Monk's brother (performed by Sterling K. Brown) is demonstrative of his desired libidinal urges. Love, sex, and pleasure are behaviors which he embraces as he familiarizes himself with his sexuality, ergo a part of himself. Acknowledging that his previous withholding of his sexuality, even from his deceased father, left sadness for him, he grasped the importance of sharing himself authentically with others. Consequently, he attempted to share his wisdom with Monk by stating, "People want to love you", thereafter providing him with an endearing kiss on the forehead. This tenderness bestowed upon Monk facilitates his awareness of the importance of a significant other in his life and asks him to challenge himself to nurture the relationship that was being cultivated.

With the various concepts to follow within a film, as the above does not capture the fullness of this film, it could leave one feeling burdened. However, the carefully woven aspects coupled with timely humor allow this film to be a brilliant source of entertainment while explicitly addressing how the use of race in art is currently held within our society.

Legacy Films

Judas and the Black Messiah (2021)

The name Judas tends to be both known and provocative notwithstanding religious affiliation. Who Judas was remains questionable. However, what is documented describes him as one of Jesus' closest disciples. Possibly an individual from the southern part of Roman Palestine, he may have been an outsider amongst the other disciples. With his treacherous behaviors influenced by Satan, he accepted thirty silver coins in exchange to identify and betray Jesus. Consequently to this decision, he became responsible for setting in motion the arrest, death by crucifixion, and resurrection of Jesus (Pruitt, 2023). It begs the question of what motives one may possess to engage in a relationship that resembles the tragic climax of this narrative. For William O'Neal, acted by LaKeith Stanfield in the film *Judas and the Black Messiah*, the similarities in the relationship he cultivated with the Black Panther Party's Chairman Fred Hampton and FBI agent Roy Mitchell were reflective of the narrative relationship of Judas and Jesus.

Mr. O'Neal being motivated by his desires to live a life free of incarceration facilitated him to become an informant to the FBI. In this circumstance, the cost of freedom was not always immediately considered. In this role he worked to provide information regarding the Black Panther Party's Chicago Branch. As this film depicts similarities to the events that occurred in the 1970s, the 1990 PBS episode "Eyes on the Prize II, An Interview with William O'Neal", filmed on April 13th, 1989, which illustrated Mr. O'Neal's personal account of being an informant, presents a narrative strikingly similar to the portrayals in the film.

Judas and the Black Messiah as well as Mr. O'Neal's interview recounting the events of his informant years shared the circumstances in which he was recruited to gain information for the FBI. Specifically, as a young adult at the age of nineteen, being in a stolen vehicle, getting into an accident across state lines, and fleeing the vehicle placed him in a criminal situation. He was identified and was made aware that incarceration was likely if charged with this crime. Alternatively, he could "join" the Black Panther Party and communicate regarding the events that took place in the organization. In an effort to sustain his freedom, Mr. O'Neal's agreement placed him in the role of an informant, a role that he notes he did not understand at the time of his consent. However, despite his lack of understanding of what becoming an informant meant, the implications of this agreement had dire consequences upon individuals, an organization, and a community.

The manner in which Mr. O'Neal engaged with both the Black Panther Party and the FBI appeared to be one of distortion. Particularly, he became a member of the party and friends with the leadership, which resulted in gaining employment as a security detail. Ironically, his security position was one that was constantly breached by his existence in the Black Panthers' space, as Mr. O'Neal was the only observed threat to the party at that time. Being within the environment with the activists, he noted he was impressed by their support, advocacy, and organization, even becoming friends with other members amongst the leadership. Mr. O'Neal was required to patronize local bars and weekly share information pertaining to the Black Panther Party's working business and personal information regarding the members with Mitchell, his FBI agent contact. His relationship with Mitchell was described as friendly, feeling that the two of them were friends rather than identifying the inherent power imbalance in the relationship, allowing the meaning and use of the word "friend" to be relative and relevant. What is a friend? One that one has a loyalty towards? One that cares for another? If these are a few of the benchmarks of friendship, then Mr. O'Neal's account of friendship from both members of the Black Panther Party as well as his FBI agent contact met the criteria in his experience. "My association with the FBI made me a better person" (William O'Neal, in PBS, 1989). And yet, in his relationship with Mitchell his "friendship" was rooted in the soil of freedom that was consistently under surveillance and compromised in the event Mr. O'Neal did not comply with requests.

But Mr. O'Neal was compliant. As a result, both organizations in which he matriculated were friendly with him, which engendered a reciprocal loyalty in the relationship while also meeting his emotional and financial needs. "Loyalty is entangled with faithfulness, endurance, selfishness, generosity, the keeping of promises" (Elshtain, 2013, p. 28). Though, Mr. O'Neal's encounters with the Black Panther Party were riddled with the significant psychological phenomenon of betrayal (Rachman, 2010). Rachman posits that "betrayal is a sense of being harmed by the intentional actions, or omissions, of a person who was assumed to be a trusted and loyal friend, relative, partner, colleague or companion" (p. 304). What tends to be disavowed and split off from awareness is the role of an informant that acts as a pawn that requires constant encouragement that can take the form of bribery and manipulation to ensure that motivations remain high enough to complete undesirable tasks. Unfortunately, and possibly in the absence of surprise, betrayal breeds "catastrophic effect(s) on the victim and psychopathological problems emerge" (Rachman, 2010, p. 304) and often causes "seemingly irreparable damage" (Johnson et al., 2001, p. 145). Such undesirable tasks and results were shared where explicit acts of betrayal of loyalties consequently led to the murder of Fred Hampton, the Black Panther Party's Chicago Branch leader.

Further, Mr. O'Neal's anxiety that manifested most times in the fear of being learned to be an informant demonstrated an internal conflict experienced in the role of being an informant that betrayed loyalties. Both loyalty and belonging appeared to be fluidly confused, where at times he regarding himself as being affiliated with the Black Panthers, for example, "When I joined The Black Panther Party"; and, other times he noted comments regarding "their organization", suggesting feeling both in and outside of the organization. And, astutely, the notable conflict is perhaps the most accurate representation of his affiliation with the FBI and the Black Panther Party. As a result, it becomes clearer the complexity of what is meant when Mr. O'Neal stated, "I was inside of the Black Panther Party looking at the movement"; "I was a part of the struggle.... At least I had a point of view. I had the courage to put it on the line. I will let history speak for me" (William O'Neal, in PBS, 1989).

108 Awaiting with Baited Breath (2020 and Beyond)

Within the film, Mr. O'Neal experienced regret, remorse, and fear, as shown in a concluding scene in the film. He begins to experience dreams of walking into chaos in the office headquarters that is in disarray and fearing his life is taken by a shooter standing unidentified in back of him before waking in a panic. On the contrary, within the documentary, his personal account indicates a lack of feeling shame for his behaviors; rather, he reported, he felt he was working with the FBI and could be proud of his contribution. Rather, the desperation to remain "free" invited the use of defense mechanisms of minimization and denial to establish and maintain a relationship with Mr. Mitchell that allowed Mr. O'Neal to be in indefinite captivity.

Luchies et al. (2010) suggest "humans have evolved to realize the wisdom of forgiving under some circumstances but not forgiving under others" (p. 734). At the conclusion of the documentary with Mr. O'Neal, the film informs that after the airing of the episode, Mr. O'Neal ended his own life by suicide. Biblically, the similarities of this life experience are great, as in Matthew 27:3–8, it is described that Judas ended his life by hanging and in another location "he burst in the midst, and all his bowels gushed out" (Acts 1:18). Whether or not there is a desire to reconcile these two verses, a common theme gleaned is that choices based upon desperation can lead to unpleasant endings, accurately depicted globally within *Judas and the Black Messiah*.

King Richard (2021)

When one has a dream that is believed with all of one's being, the image of its truth is imprinted and is unwavering. Logic and rational thought may suggest that the chances of the dream becoming reality are slender; however, a tether holds the dream for it to remain. Richard Williams (performed by Will Smith), the father of tennis champions Venus and Serena Williams, possessed a dream that his two unborn daughters would become tennis athletes, winners of cups, and the best of all time. With his dream and perseverance, he offered the family the possibility of freedom of choice and freedom from future financial stressors.

Within *King Richard*, Mr. Williams is portrayed as an individual who has a strong presence and will. He readily believes in the fate of his daughters, grooming them for athletic greatness while valuing their education and citizenship and fostering their ability to enjoy their childhood. He believes that if allowed to be well-rounded individuals in concert with their extraordinary tennis talents, they will be grounded and able to withstand the stardom that they are destined to achieve. To that end, Mr. Williams understands that their youth and global development are as important as nurturing their talents. In doing so, he protected his children from threats and concerns of exploitation, which many times landed as oppositional and unprofessional with coaches, thus creating ruptures within his professional relationships. His protection of his children allowed him to have the courage to confront neighborhood male youth and deter them from making advances towards his daughters. His belief in his dream placed him in vulnerable situations where he was physically assaulted by said male youth on numerous occasions at the neighborhood tennis court where he trained his daughters. For fear that physical assaults will continue to occur, he intends to confront the youth with a gun brandished. Prior to any confrontation, he witnesses the male become a victim of a drive-by shooting that kills him. This scene not only highlights the dedication he had towards ensuring he had space to foster his dream on behalf of his daughters, but the violence within his environment that was ever present and from which his dream promised a means of escape.

Mr. Williams cultivated his dream for his daughters continuously. His protection of his dream required every family member to hold a trust in him to make proper decisions regarding the family's future along with training opportunities for both Venus and Serena Williams. He was successfully able to share what he saw for his children and engaged the entire family to support his vision. To ensure they also had a clear vision, he concretized the success that they would have, driving the family through wealthy neighborhoods in his aged van allowing them to choose homes of interest and interact with the fantasy of purchasing, living in, and redesigning the home in a manner that met their fancy. With confidence he assured his daughters that their success would render them any home wherever they desired.

Due to the family's diligence, Mr. Williams' dreams for his two daughters were predictions of their future. His understanding of the talents his daughters possessed and the influence they would have both in the world of tennis and across the world globally was spot on. Might Richard Williams have recognized his spirit in the work of Dalton et al. (2016) who posited that it is possible to break financial distress by altering aspirations alone? Mr. Williams was aware that in the absence of a dream children can "end up on these streets", a proposition he refused for them. His safeguarding against that option included steadfast focus that engaged a regimented training schedule and abundant family involvement.

Within his paternal role, Mr. Williams' dedication to conceptualizing the needs of his daughters, the risks taken to gain access and privileges for them, and the physical and emotional protection offered to his children lead to an idealized presentation. However, the film bravely adds to Mr. Williams' character by offering an integrated view of his humanity. In concert with the aforementioned points, illustrations of his struggle to be a partner in his marriage are shared. Admission to a lack of relationship with his children from a previous relationship and how his dedication to his children's success frequently resulted in a rigidity that hindered his ability to allow other persons' perspectives in for consideration were also highlighted. The manner in which we arrive to the destination in one's dream is curved with pebbles and obstructions that can create doubt and discontinue the journey. However, Mr. Williams' unconventional methods of achieving for the benefit of his family were unparalleled, making what he was able to bestow upon them priceless.

Respect (2021)

The life of Aretha Franklin was one of poise, grace, fight, and extraordinary talent. Within the film *Respect* (2021), the narrative follows a young Aretha (acted by Skye Dakota Turner), a child of divorced parents, and the experiences that were salient in making the artist that is beloved. Initially, as a young girl, Aretha was depicted as a child who loves her mother who was a singer. She adores her and she appears to feel adored by her. Belonging to an upper-middle-class family with a pastor for a father placed emphasis on etiquette and propriety. Aretha was eloquent, careful with words, and pleasant. Within her early childhood, her father perceived her to have vocal talent that would blossom into greatness. As a result, he nurtured her vocal talents and encouraged her to sing for adults at parties he hosted. He adored Aretha and she exhibited a similar love and respect for him. Though, Aretha's youth was short-lived. At the age of ten, her mother died of a heart attack, resulting in her residing full time in the care of her father and paternal grandmother. Her mother prior to her death informed Aretha that no one owned her voice but her. This event was such a tragedy that Aretha became selectively mute and unable to both communicate and sing. Within the film's account, her father grew impatient and demanded she resume utilizing her voice. She concedes and begins to speak and sing again once she is told by her vocal instructor and her father's church confidant that music had the potential to save one's life. Though a sheltered child with a careful watch on her voice and performance, Aretha experienced events that became the catalyst for emotional grievances that haunted her well into adulthood.

Freud's drive theory posits "that if a child is either overfrustrated or overgratified at an early psychosexual stage (as per the interaction of the child's constitutional endowment and the parents' responsiveness), he or she would become 'fixated' on the issues of that stage" (McWilliams, 2011, p. 23). Withholding, a behavior typically utilized within the anal phase within one's development, acts as a way to be able to exert control over oneself and the environment around one. While Aretha's voice was managed by her father throughout her early childhood, she was possibly overgratified with laud, yet overfrustrated by the death of her mother that rendered her temporarily mute for a prolonged amount of time. In her adolescent and emerging adult years, her level of autonomy was frequently challenged by her father and was encouraged to remain limited to his guidance. Though he protected her vocally in her career, he struggles to emotionally protect her, specifically from predators in her environment. Consequently, Aretha does not confide in her family when she is exposed to sexual behaviors nor does she disclose the father of her two children when she becomes pregnant at twelve and fourteen years of age.

In adulthood, Ms. Franklin's unresolved pain resulted in a great deal of emotional consequences. Her use of defenses that were well entrenched, such as repression, allowed her to not recall specifics of her past. In particular, she learns that her memory of her parents' volatile relationship characterized by her siblings as a relationship with frequent arguments was outside of her awareness. Rather, she appeared surprised by the information they provided her and how her parents' relationship resembled the relationship she had with her husband. Her successful use of this particular defense of repression positioned her in a space that not only made her truth unrevealing to her, but also made her past inaccessible to her to inform her present decisions.

Further, the act of Ms. Franklin's withholding tended to manifest in a manner that caused her to turn her pain inward. Bouts of depression haunted her where she engaged in heavy use of alcohol consumption, resulting in paranoia that suggested others would betray her and be unable to understand her responsibilities.

Indeed, Ms. Franklin's secrets were laid to rest with her in death. She never satisfied the curiosities that her loved ones and others had regarding the father of her first two born children. She did not disclose the nature of their relationship. It is unclear whether she ever recalled the quality of her parents' relationship when she was a young child as within the film this aspect remained unresolved. Though, Ms. Franklin sang regarding her desires of respect and this film is astutely named in its honor. Respect may have been what she desired, and in her lifetime she reaped in scores.

Till (2022)

"Freedom for everyone or freedom fails."

Mrs. Mamie Till-Mobley

Mrs. Mamie Till-Mobley noted in her speech humbly that she was wrong to believe that the events that happened in the South in America were not her business as a resident of Chicago. As a result of the lynching of her son, Emmett Till, she began to understand that the events that happen to African Americans everywhere are everyone's business. Prior to visiting family in Mississippi, Mrs. Till offered warnings to her son Emmett regarding the nature of hate towards African Americans in the South in the 1950s. Communication suggested that when visiting the South one's freedom to be demonstrative of oneself as a Black person must be tapered, and withheld. Albeit, there is no real way to do so due to one's visible melanin skin; however, the goal was noted to behave in a humble manner, ultimately placing White individuals at ease without creating offense. One mistake, one wrong move and the consequences could be dire. Mrs. Till's anxieties regarding her son's visit to spend time with his family were warranted. Bidding him farewell at the train station in Chicago with a gripping hug would be the last time she would see him alive.

The history of Emmett Till coupled with the force his death had on the push for civil rights is widely known. His death resulting from his encounter with Mrs. Bryant at a convenience store led her to allege that he had been sexually and physically intrusive towards her and that this had resulted in his kidnapping, brutal murder, and body being found in the Tallahatchie River attached to a cotton gin fan with barbed wire. Once found, his bloated, disfigured body was sent to Chicago for burial where his mother insisted on having an open casket (now housed in a dark alcove of the Smithsonian's National Museum of African American History and Culture) to show the world what had happened to her son.

In addition to the compromised freedom of an African American in the South at that time, the history of Emmett Till equally demonstrates a phenomenon that continues to occur within present time. The limited freedoms of being a Black boy in the United States perpetuate where individuals view Black boys as older and therefore these boys are held responsible for their actions as adults in both casual and legal environments far more readily than their White counterparts. Notably, within the legal transcript of Mrs. Bryant's testimony in Tallahatchie County Circuit Court on September 22nd, 1955, she referred to Emmett Till by the "N" word and described him as a "man". Emmett Till, a fourteen year old, was described as "a man" rather than as the adolescent he was at the time of the incident and his death. Research findings published by the American Psychological Association by Goff et al. (2014) found that White individuals tend to view African American boys as young as ten years of age to be less innocent than their White peers and their age tends to be overestimated by approximately four and a half years. Co-author of Goff et al. (2014), Matthew Jackson, Ph.D. noted, "With the average age overestimation for black boys exceeding four-and-a-half years, in some cases, black children may be viewed as adults when they are just 13 years old", a similar dynamic to that found in Mrs. Bryant's testimony of the fourteen-year-old Emmett Till.

Roy Bryant and his brother-in-law J.W. Milam who were charged with the murder of Emmett Till were unsurprisingly (based upon Mrs. Bryant's testimony and the twelve segregated, middle-aged, White male jurors) acquitted. In 1956, within an article in *Look Magazine*, both Roy Bryant and J.W. Milam admitted to murdering Emmett Till but they could not be retried. Later, Carolyn Bryant Donham spoke to Timothy B. Tyson, a Duke University professor, writer, and historian. Pérez-Peña's (2017) article regarding Tyson's book, *The Blood of Emmett Till*, reported that Tyson cites that within an interview with Mrs. Bryant Donham she acknowledged, "her long-ago allegations that Emmett grabbed her and was menacing and sexually crude toward her, [that part is not true]"—an admission of perjury.

"The violent and unexpected death of a child is an experience that time does not heal completely. Invisible wounds remain, and individuals are left to face the traumatic aspects of the loss for many years" (Essakow & McInnes Miller, 2013, p. 307). Emmett Till's heinous death in the 1950s resulted in The Emmett Till Anti-Lynching Act being signed into law by President Joe Biden on March 29th, 2022. These laws that are created to provide safety to citizens have unfortunately not deterred individuals from hunting Black boys and men in the streets without sound reason. As a result, in 2024 we are exposed to films shot by mobile phones and body cameras of police officers. These rough cuts with choppy sound and aggressive visual movements that capture a person of color being chased, tased, shot, and killed by persons in authority frequent news channels all too often. Being kind to audiences, we are provided the warning that the content about to be seen may be disturbing to some to watch—suggesting that watching the killing of a Black person is not disturbing to all. These films accomplish Ms. Till's mother's wishes, for the world to see what is happening. As we now have the opportunity to see what is happening, it now can be everyone's business. And because of this, we can recognize the meaning of why Black Lives Matter remains a resisting force. It is the hope that, seventy years after Emmett Till's death, here in America freedom can ultimately equate to safety.

Final Thoughts

Every writing piece requires an offering of one's heart, personality, and soul. The development of this book required nothing less from me. At the onset of writing, there was an overwhelming amount of excitement to share the intersection of psychology and film with an engaging audience. I hoped that this book would allow an opportunity to have a greater understanding of the history of psychology's interest in film coupled with African American cinema over the years. The development of this book provided the best reasons to watch classic films that have undergirded African American culture.

Once beginning to view these films, I became acutely aware of the journey I was inviting readers to embark upon. The films being reviewed were evocative, provocative even, eliciting intense feelings and profound existential thought. Constructing this book elucidated an awareness that the films of my history were instrumental in shaping my conceptualization of the world and individuals within it. The Friday evenings at the theaters I made reference to in the introduction were saturated with films of trauma narratives, illustrating perpetrators and victims, lives that were both similar to and dissimilar from my daily lived experience as an adolescent. My ability to relate to the characters and themes was not personal; yet, I was aware that if consciously desired, the experiences on screen were not out of reach. I understood, within those adolescent years, that personal decisions were being made to have and maintain a life with friends, opportunities, and limited traumatic exposures. I also knew those decisions were a result of privileges I possessed. Thus, the idea of privilege, before it became a necessary diversity and equity buzzword, was a concept that was present and worked to be protected.

Watching films at a specific developmental age also had its consequences. With the goal of being entertained on a Friday night, in the content to which I was exposed were concepts that were both mature and influential. Rewatching these films for this book elucidated the amount of information that had originally gone over my head when I saw these art pieces again. Admittedly, I was astonished by how much information I did not recall, either because it was not picked up on, I was ill-equipped to process the information due to a lack of knowledge or experience, or because the content required my adolescent self to defend by using denial, repression, or suppression to cope with certain material. I can recall attempting to utilize

DOI: 10.4324/9781003399902-8

reaction formations, a defense mechanism in my youth, to cope with film content I screened. Those reaction formations encouraged me to determine that environments in which individuals navigated could be somehow achieved out of by gaining education, working hard, and pursuing the American dream. My naivety did not afford me to consider systemic racism and oppression as causes that perpetuated lack of freedoms. Now, decades and a score later, I see these films diligently showcased these societal issues making them all the more impactful. The film *Boyz N the Hood* (1991) has always been a beloved feature and I believe highlights this point explicitly. Whether viewed when I was an adolescent or as an adult, the film is held in mind for days after with thoughts and many questions. The sobering bereft tones of *Boyz N the Hood*'s soundtrack, specifically Stanley Clarke's "Black on Black Crime", always were evocative, swaddling scenes in an ominous hold. Unsurprisingly, engrossing one so deeply into the psychological experience of the film means these tones become magnified as they haunt—leaving the heartbreaking reality that this tale reflects the life of many who reside in communities riddled with violence and hardships here in America. And despite knowing and caring about what goes on in the hood, the traumatic challenges faced can feel insurmountable given the insidious nature of systemic influences.

Now, as an adult with some knowing and hopefully greater consciousness, free will was used during the creation of this book. Understanding the impact film has upon one's psyche, there are movie selections that I screened for this book which I imagine I will not call myself to screen again. For example, when watching the film *Detroit* after screening numerous films documenting the struggle of African American individuals to obtain civil rights, I found myself in two places at once: the familiar and the unfamiliar. I felt the familiar psychodynamic theories begin to surface. Psychological effects of being assaulted, fear for one's own and others' lives, and, as a result of these events, observing the numerous trauma responses that were experienced thereafter were initial areas of psychological note. The physiological shaking, sweating, and the emotional terror the teens experienced on the evening of July 23rd, 1967 were nothing less than horrific. Folk psychologists, as earlier defined as "film spectators, filmmakers, critics, and scholars, untutored and intuitive psychology" (Plantinga, 2011, p. 26), could see the writing on these walls and despite how astute it was, no psychological interpretation seemed necessary. Rather, it felt important that such a film was understood purely in its current state without using psychological concepts to further glean what was being seen. Emotional torture, abuse of power, and visceral vulnerability needed no further explanation. Rather than having the opportunity to explore what could have been, perhaps contemplating the developmental time of emerging adulthood and all of its wonders for example, inhumane treatment by officials with a counterbalance of officials that varied in benevolence were alternatively provided in this film and sadly in the reality of the events that occurred on those two days. I also positioned myself in the unfamiliar, speechless—feeling that there lacked theories to add meaningfully to what was portrayed. I concluded that the turbulence of adolescence and finding oneself during emerging adulthood is effortful. Though there are many tales offered that describe adolescent angst that include forms of non-compliance and rebellion, the results of being held in captivity as a hostage are less explored, resulting in the contribution in this book (p. 000). Recognizing the importance of sharing the content of these films with audiences, I felt I consciously was required to balance the fatigue of continuing to explore similar psychological dynamics in films over and over again.

And, my free will has also charged me to be protective of my psyche. Films I screened in the past I cannot say I will ever view again, and could not even in the service of this book. Though countless films were unfortunately not included in this piece of literature, certain films were excluded with great contemplative purpose, for example, *New Jack City* (1991). *New Jack City* (1991), directed by Mario Van Peebles and starring Wesley Snipes, Ice-T, Chris Rock, Mario Van Peebles, Allen Payne, and Judd Asher Nelson, depicts the drug enterprise of Nino Brown and his dealings in Harlem, New York City during the crack cocaine epidemic while an undercover NYPD officer attempts to close his business and end the power he has over the residential neighborhoods. I have seen this film twice in its entirety. The first time I watched this film was in the year of its release. The recollection I have of myself viewing the film is one of me frozen. Watching the film again years later, in hopes that my age and maturity would dampen my response, only made the same images that were imprinted in my mind further inculcated. Admittedly, speaking about and to this film remains psychologically curtailing. Fragmented thoughts and feelings are all I can offer to the psychological currents of this film. To add this film to this piece of literature would have been a disservice to you the reader. To watch this film again would have been a disservice to myself—a psychological burden I felt I could not shoulder, even for the birth of this book, and I imagine for any future pieces I craft. Screenwriters Thomas Lee Wright and Barry Michael Cooper and director Mario Van Peebles created such a compelling tale illustrated in this film; and, though I imagine I will never sit to view this film again, the work will remain with me for a lifetime.

Understandably, individuals reading this who are familiar with the films within this book may feel similarly regarding other films. Indeed, sometimes watching a film once is enough and it will be forever present in who they are. Films such as *The Color Purple* (1988), *12 Years a Slave* (2012), *Till* (2022), *Menace II Society* (1993), and *Boys N the Hood* (1991) may be a few of these films where the maltreatment and violence that occur in these cinematic works are so great that it is hard to view once, and grows ever more difficult when viewing multiple times. The love depicted by the women in *The Color Purple*, the perseverance and resilience demonstrated in *12 Years a Slave*, and the highly sophisticated defense mechanism of sublimation Ms. Till demonstrated could persuade one to watch these films again if desired, possibly. Yet, *Menace II Society* (1993) fell into the position of a film I would never view again. When I was in the rows of the theater upon its release, as was typical, I was happy to support black art. Yet, I walked out of the theater when I felt the content was overstimulating. Now, watching as an adult, the content remains overstimulating, yet I can place in perspective the lessons that viewers are asked to internalize in making choices for oneself as an adult.

And now, I would like to take a moment of gratitude, which is always appropriate and needed. Thank you for love. Thank the heavens and the Lord for films such as *Love Jones* (1997), *Love and Basketball* (2000), and more recently *The Photograph* (2020). These beloved characters that felt over time like friends shared narratives that were stories that happened to be performed by a black cast rather than being a black film. For those who question whether there is a difference, at this time in my journey of understanding psychology and film, I believe there is a distinction between the two. Films such as *Brown Sugar* (2002) (not included) and *The Best Man* (1999) for examples exhibited passionate love that encompassed one's career, friendship, and love of self and provided clarity on the ways to passionately love another, all while sophisticatedly infusing black culture by music, clothing, and dialect, making these films poetically and psychologically healing art pieces of their time.

The Yellow Brick Road to Hollywood

"No racial group or ethnicity was more blatantly distorted than African Americans" within cinematic history (Bogle, 2019, p. 2). The history of moviemaking is long with complex hardship, motivation for progress, change, and perseverance in the filmmaking industry. I wish I could state that the fight African Americans face in cinema and within America has come to its conclusion—to be truly represented and respected as fellow humans in all environments. That desire is a utopia that exists where African Americans in all industries are treated, considered, and compensated in the same manner as their white counterparts without contemplation and with consistency. These mainstream films would include a diverse set of roles available that accurately reflects the human condition of those of color in America in the absence of familiar racial tropes to comfort viewers, or these tropes would be explicitly addressed as such. We continue to lack the ability to ease on down the road as there remain potholes, places in need of repair, and in some spaces the road remains under construction. We have learned to use resources to create detours that have allowed some to arrive to destinations by winning awards most coveted for their cinematic contributions. As the tool Twitter was used in 2015 by April Reign to highlight the continued energy needed in the efforts of diversity and equity by using the hashtag OscarsSoWhite, this acknowledges that one influential body, the Academy of Motion Picture Arts and Sciences, continued to struggle to recognize films created by and featuring African American artists. Given the spaces African Americans occupy, the need for such a hashtag usage revealed the glaring difference between movement and progress when it comes to equity and inclusion.

Acknowledging the accomplishments of gifted filmmakers and their contribution to culture creation from 1895 to the 1970s, the infancy and adolescent years of moving pictures, we can be inspired and students of how we have understood who we have been, where we are, and where we dream to be. Bringing us to today, there have been specific filmmakers who have not only gathered the golden bricks necessary to create the paths into the industry, but who engineered them by using their natural and nurtured talents to mason roads forging ways for themselves and current artists. In doing so, we have had filmmakers and actors who have achieved industry and public greatness—fame, financial wealth, and collegial recognition for their body of work. Lena Horne, Sydney Poitier, Hattie McDaniel, Denzel Washington, Viola Davis, Halle Berry, Barry Jenkins, Roger Ross Williams, Morgan Freeman, Cuba Gooding, Jr., Daniel Kaluuya, Mahershala Ali, Ava DuVernay, Cord Jefferson, and more continue to hold a torch and create a blaze for individuals to follow. Their expertise within their craft both opens doors and equally provides a model for others to know what they too can achieve within the film industry and offer audiences. Their sheer vision, dedication, initiative, and persistence to create art that represents African American people ensure representations exist to accurately depict African Americans and African American culture in film. For decades, these films have had the power to live on in the psyche of their viewers, influencing the understanding of the human condition for African American communities, within this nation and beyond.

Special Thanks

Thank you to my Creator and Savior for bestowing upon me these words and ideas to share with others. Thank you for placing the following people and institutions in my path to make this publication possible. To my parents who have provided me unwavering academic and intellectual support and instilled in me that all I dream is possible. An additional thank you to my mother who was my first editor to the pages that I have the opportunity to share with you. To Pepper who always has faith in any endeavor I attempt and supports the firmest and cheers the loudest. To my sisters, Aisha and Bonita; thank you for reminding me of who I am and loving me through who I would like to become. Ezinna, thank you for being a sister friend and a member of "my team". Thank you to my supportive sister Maia. To Lisa, my sister who enlightens me upon Katwalks. I appreciate this time with you more than you know. To Lara, thank you for keeping me in mind and championing for me to further my pursuits. Thank you Loring. Your astute perceptions many times reassured and revealed aspects of myself to me that I am happy to have become acquainted with. Please know that your support helps allow my professional growth to be more efficient and a journey of both self-discovery and self-acceptance. The George Washington University's Psychodynamic Film and Media Set for their commitment to conceptualizing psychodynamic concepts within films and interest in furthering research within this arena. A special thank you to Ms. Shea Baggett, your enthusiasm coupled with your research labors was a privilege to work with. To the National Museum of African American History and Culture for their committed installation of *Taking the Stage* that recognizes the powerful African American creatives within the art of film. Thank you to The Academy Museum for featuring the history of African American film in the *Regeneration: Black Cinema 1898–1971* exhibit. Thank you for sharing your experiences and memories with such vulnerability Mr. Marvin Chambers, Mrs. Tasha Winns Carter, Mr. Simeone Deskins, Dr. Paris Gasque, Dr. Tanesha Handy Lloyd, Ms. Nicole Nichols, Dr. Anthony Perdue, Mr. Jason Saunders, and Mr. Darryl Thompson.

And forever, to my beloved mentor, Richard Ruth, Ph.D., who saw me kindly and gently shepherded me into my career dreams.

Bibliography

Academy Museum. (2023). *Regeneration: Black cinema 1898–1971* [Exhibition]. Academy Museum of Motion Pictures, Los Angeles, CA, United States.

Alexander, C. S. (2019). Forget Mammy!: Blaxploitation's deconstruction of the classic film trope with black feminism, black power, and "bad" voodoo mamas. *The Journal of Popular Culture, 52*(4), 839–860.

American Psychological Association. (2014). Black boys viewed as older, less innocent than whites, research finds. Washington, DC: APA. https://www.apa.org/news/press/releases/2014/03/black-boys-older.

American Psychological Association (APA). (2018a). Sublimation. *APA Dictionary of Psychology*. Washington, DC: APA. https://dictionary.apa.org/sublimation.

American Psychological Association (APA). (2018b). Escapism. *APA Dictionary of Psychology*. Washington, DC: APA. https://dictionary.apa.org/escapism.

Anderson, D. D. (1992). Using feature films as tools for analysis in a psychology and law course. *Teaching of Psychology, 19*(3), 155–158.

Andy (History of Africa Podcast). (2023, January 12). The Woman King's historical lies: why they matter. *Ordinary Times*. https://ordinary-times.com/2023/01/12/historical-revisionism-and-the-woman-king/#:~:text=The%20problem%20with%20The%20Woman,in%20depictions%20of%20African%20history.

ANON, The Griot. (2019, June 13). Moment of clarity. https://www.anonthegriot.com/post/celebrities-are-humans-too-15-awkward-moments-you-have-to-see.

Avildsen, J. G. (Director). (1989). *Lean on Me* [Film]. Warner Bros.

Baldwin, J. (1974). *If Beale Street Could Talk.* New York, NY: The Dial Press.

Benedetti, F. (2021). Placebos and movies: What do they have in common? *Current Directions in Psychological Science, 30*(3), 274–279. https://doi.org/10.1177/09637214211003892.

Bernhart, M. (2021). 'What do you think it is that makes them who they are'? The connections between Latinx stereotypes, claims of white difference, and characters' deaths in *Breaking Bad. Critical Studies in Television: The International Journal of Television Studies, 16*(3), 245–263. https://doi.org/10.1177/17496020211023865.

Bible, New King James Version (NKJV). (2023).

Bigelow, K. (Director). (2017). *Detroit* [Film]. Annapurna Pictures.

Bird, H. (2017). Out of the shadows. *Community Practitioners, 90*(3), 37–39.

Black, M. C., Basile, K. C., Breiding, M. J., Smith, S. G., Walters, M. L., Merrick, M. T., Chen, J., & Stevens, M. R. (2011). *The National Intimate Partner and Sexual Violence Survey (NISVS): 2010 Summary Report.* Atlanta, GA: National Center for Injury Prevention and Control, Centers for Disease Control and Prevention.

Bluestone, C. (2000). Feature films as a teaching tool. *College Teaching, 48*(4), 141–146. https://doi.org/10.1080/87567550009595832.

Bogle, D. (2019). *Hollywood Black. The Stars, the Films, the Filmmakers.* Philadelphia, PA: Running Press.

Boissoneault, L. (2017, October 6). The true story behind "Marshall". *Smithsonian Magazine.* https://www.smithsonianmag.com/history/true-story-behind-marshall-180965148/.

Bolt, M. (1976). Using films based on literature in teaching psychology. *Teaching Psychology, 3*(4), 189–190.

Box Office Mojo. (2022). Domestic yearly box office. https://www.boxofficemojo.com/year/ytd/.

Box Office Mojo. (2024). Domestic yearly box office. https://www.boxofficemojo.com/year/ytd/.

Boyd, B. (2009). *On the Origin of Stories: Evolution, Cognition, and Fiction.* Cambridge, MA: Harvard University Press.

Brewer, C. (Director). (2005). *Hustle and Flow* [Film]. Paramount Pictures.

Brooks, S. K., & Greenberg, N. (2021). Psychological impact of being wrongfully accused of criminal offences. A systemic literature review. *Medicine, Science and the Law, 61*(1), 44–54.

Bucciferro, C. (2021). Representations of gender and race in Ryan Coogler's film *Black Panther*: Disrupting Hollywood tropes. *Critical Studies in Media Communication, 38*(2), 169–182. DOI: 10.1111/jpcu.12830.

Cameron, M. (2008). The effect of loss of a child on subsequent parenting. Paper presented at the annual meeting of the American Sociological Association, Boston, MA.

Carr, S. (Director). (2000). *Next Friday* [Film]. New Line Cinema.

Carveth, D. (2010). Superego, conscience, and the nature and types of guilt. *Modern Psychoanalysis, 35*(1), 106–130.

Carveth, D. (2016). Why we should stop conflating the superego with the conscience. *Psychoanalysis, Culture & Society, 22*(1), 15–32.

Castle, N. (Director). (1989). *Tap* [Film]. TriStar Pictures.

Chukwu, C. (Director). (2022). *Till* [Film]. United Artists Releasing (America) & Universal Pictures.

Cohen, A. J. (2002). Music cognition and the cognitive psychology of film structure. *Canadian Psychology, 43*(4), 215–232.

Cohen, A. J. (2005). How music influences the interpretation of film and video: Approaches from experimental psychology. In R. A. Kendall & R. W. H. Savage (Eds.), *Perspectives in Systematic Musicology* (pp. 15–36). Los Angeles: UCLA Ethnomusicology Publications.

Cohen, J. (2001). Defining identification: A theoretical look at the identification of audiences with media characters. *Mass Communication and Society, 4*(3), 245–264.

Condon, B. (Director). (2006). *Dreamgirls* [Film]. DreamWorks Pictures & Paramount Pictures.

Coogler, R. (Director). (2018). *Black Panther* [Film]. Walt Disney Studios Motion Pictures.

Coogler, R. (Director). (2022). *Black Panther: Wakanda Forever* [Film]. Walt Disney Studios Motion Pictures.

Cupchik, G. C. (2001). Aesthetics and emotion in entertainment media. *Media Psychology, 3*(1), 69–89. DOI: 10.1207/S1532785XMEP0301_04.

Currie, G. (2004). Cognitivism. In T. Miller & R. Stam (Eds.), *A Companion to Film Theory* (pp. 105–122). Oxford: Wiley-Blackwell.

122 Bibliography

Cutting, J. E. (2007). Perceiving scenes in film and in the world. In J. D. Anderson & B. Fisher Anderson (Eds.), *Moving Image Theory: Ecological Considerations* (pp. 9–27). Carbondale, IL: Southern Illinois University Press.

Dalton, P. S., Ghosal, S., & Mani, A. (2016). Poverty and aspirations failure. *The Economic Journal*, *126*(590), 165–188.

David, E. J. R., Schroeder, T. M., & Fernandez, J. (2019). Internalized racism: A systematic review of the psychology literature on racism's most insidious consequence. *Journal of Social Issues*, *75*(4), 1057–1086.

David, F. (2015). When it comes to modern slavery, do definitions matter? *Anti-Trafficking Review*, (5), 150–152.

de Leeuw, R. N. H., & Buijzen, M. (2016). Introducing positive media psychology to the field of children, adolescents and media. *Journal of Children and Media*, *10*(1), 39–46. https://doi.org/10.1080/17482798.2015.1121892.

DeMarco, D. (2015). Too late for regret. *Human Life Review*, *41*(4), 55–60.

Després, C. (1991). The meaning of home: Literature review and directions for future research and theoretical development. *Journal of Architectural and Planning Research*, *8*(2), 96–115.

Dickerson, E. (Director). (1992). *Juice* [Film]. Paramount Pictures & 20th Century Home Entertainment.

Dost, A., & Yagmurlu, B. (2008). Are constructiveness and destructiveness essential features of guilt and shame feelings respectively? *Journal for the Theory of Social Behaviour*, *38*(2), 109–129.

Duncan, L. (2020). The psychology of protests and activism, with Lauren Duncan. *Speaking of Psychology*, Ep. 108. https://www.apa.org/news/podcasts/speaking-of-psychology/protest-activism.

DuVernay, A. (Director). (2014). *Selma* [Film]. Paramount Pictures (American) & 20th Century Fox (International).

Easton, D., & Hardy, J. (1997). *The Ethical Slut. A Practice Guide to Polyamory, Open Relationships & Other Adventures.* New York: Crown Publishing Group.

Elshtain, J. B. (2013). On loyalty. *First Things: A Monthly Journal of Religion and Public Life*, (235), 27–31.

Eschholz, S., Bufkin, J., & Long, J. (2002). Symbolic reality bites: Women and racial/ethnic minorities in modern film. *Sociological Spectrum*, *22*(3), 299–334. DOI: 10.1080/02732170290062658.

Essakow, K. L., & McInnes Miller, M. (2013). Piecing together the shattered heirloom: Parents' experience of relationship resilience after the violent death of a child. *The American Journal of Family Therapy*, *41*(4), 299–310.

Famuyiwa, R. (Director). (1999). *The Wood* [Film]. Paramount Pictures.

Famuyiwa, R. (Director). (2002). *Brown Sugar* [Film]. Paramount Pictures.

Fleming, M. Z., Piedmont, R. L., & Hiam, C. M. (1990). Images of madness: Feature films in teaching psychology. *Teaching of Psychology*, *17*(3), 185–187.

Foner, P. S. (Ed.). (1999). *Frederick Douglass: Selected Speeches and Writings*. Chicago, IL: Lawrence Hill.

Freud, S. (1923). *The Ego and the Id.* Standard Edition, vol. 19 (pp. 1–66). London: Hogarth Press.

Freud, S., McLintock, D., & Haughton, H. (2003). *The Uncanny*. London: Penguin Classics.

Furie, S. (Director). (1972). *Lady Sings the Blues* [Film]. Paramount Pictures.

Bibliography 123

Gabbard, G. (2005). *Psychodynamic Psychiatry in Clinical Practice* (4th ed.). Washington, DC: American Psychiatric Publishing, Inc.

Germeys, F., & d'Ydewalle, G. (2007). The psychology of film: Perceiving beyond the cut. *Psychological Research, 71*(4), 458–466. DOI: 10.1007/s00426-005-0025-3.

Gibson, B. (Director). (1993). *What's Love Got to Do with It* [Film]. Touchstone Pictures.

Gillum, T. L. (2002). Exploring the link between stereotypic images and intimate partner violence in the African American community. *Violence Against Women, 8*(1), 64–86. https://doi.org/10.1177/10778010222182946.

Goff, P. A., Jackson, M. C., Di Leone, B. A. L., Culotta, C. M., & DiTomasso, N. A. (2014). The essence of innocence: Consequences of dehumanizing black children. *Journal of Personality and Social Psychology, 106*(4), 526–545.

Gooden, W. E. (1980). *The Adult Development of Black Men* (Vols. 1 & 2). Ann Arbor, MI: University Microfilms.

Gray, F. G. (Director). (1995). *Friday* [Film]. New Line Cinema.

Gray, F. G. (Director). (1996). *Set It Off* [Film]. New Line Cinema.

Green, R. M. (Director). (2021). *King Richard* [Film]. Warner Brothers Pictures.

Hampton, R., Oliver, W., & Magarian, L. (2003). Domestic violence in the African American community: An analysis of social and structural factors. *Violence Against Women, 9*(5), 533–557. https://doi.org/10.1177/1077801202250450.

Henschel, A., & McDevitt-Murphy, M. E. (2016). How do aftermath of battle experiences affect returning OEF/OIF veterans? *Military Behavioral Health, 4*(4), 345–350. https://doi.org/10.1080/21635781.2016.1181583.

Herman, J. (1992). *Trauma and Recovery: The Aftermath of Violence – from Domestic Abuse to Political Trauma.* New York: Basic Books.

Hill, J. (Director). (1974). *Foxy Brown* [Film]. American International Pictures.

Hockenbury, D. H., & Hockenbury, S. E. (2008). *Psychology* (5th ed.). New York: Worth Publishers.

hooks, b. (1992). *Black Looks: Race and Representation.* Boston, MA: South End Press.

Hopper, D. (Director). (1988). *Colors* [Film]. Orion Pictures.

Howell, E. (2020). *Trauma and Dissociation-Informed Psychotherapy.* New York: W.W. Horton & Company.

Howell, K. H., Thurston, I. B., Schwartz, L. E., Jamison, L. E., & Hasselle, A. J. (2018). Protective factors associated with resilience in women exposed to intimate partner violence. *Psychology of Violence, 8*(4), 438–447. https://doi.org/10.1037/vio0000147.

Howell, R. (2011). Lights, camera…action? Altered attitudes and behaviour in response to the climate change film *The Age of Stupid. Global Environmental Change, 21*(1), 177–187.

Hudlin, R. (Director). (1992). *Boomerang* [Film]. Paramount Pictures.

Hughes, A., & Hughes, A. (Directors). (1993). *Menace to Society* [Film]. New Line Cinema.

Hughes, A., & Hughes, A. (Directors). (1995). *Dead Presidents* [Film]. Hollywood Pictures, Walt Disney Studios Motion Pictures.

Jefferson, C. (Director). (2023). *American Fiction* [Film]. Orion Pictures/Amazon MGM Studios.

Jenkins, B. (Director). (2016). *Moonlight* [Film]. A24.

Jenkins, B. (Director). (2018). *If Beale Street Could Talk* [Film]. Annapurna Pictures.

Jerald, M. C., Ward, L. M., Moss, L., Thomas, K., & Fletcher, K. D. (2017). Subordinates, sex objects, or Sapphires? Investigating contributions of media use to black students' femininity ideologies and stereotypes about black women. *Journal of Black Psychology, 43*(6), 608–635. https://doi.org/10.1177/0095798416665967.

124 Bibliography

Jewison, N. (Director). (1984). *A Soldier's Story* [Film]. Columbia Pictures.

Joel, S., MacDonald, G., & Plaks, J. E. (2012). Attachment anxiety uniquely predicts regret proneness in close relationship contexts. *Social Psychology and Personality Science*, *3*(3), 348–355.

Johnson, S. M., Makinen, J. A., & Millikin, J. W. (2001). Attachment injuries in couple relationships: A new perspective on impasses in couples therapy. *Journal of Marital and Family Therapy*, *27*(2), 145–155.

Kashani, T. (2015). *Movies Change Lives: Pedagogy of Constructive Humanistic Transformation Through Cinema (Minding the Media)*. New York, NY: Peter Lang Publishing.

Kelly, J. F., & Greene, B. (2010). Diversity within African American, female therapists: Variability in clients' expectations and assumptions about the therapist. *Psychotherapy: Theory, Research, Practice, Training*, *47*(2), 186–197. https://doi.org/10.1037/a0019759.

Kimble Wrye, H. (2009). The fourth wave of feminism: Psychoanalytic perspectives introductory remarks. *Studies in Gender and Sexuality*, *10*(4), 185–189. DOI: 10.1080/15240650903227999.

King, P. M. (Director). (2008). *Sex and the City* [Film]. New Line Productions.

King, S. (Director). (2021). *Judas and the Black Messiah* [Film]. Warner Brothers Pictures.

Kinney, D. K. (1975). Cinema thrillers: Reviews of films highly rated by psychology students. *Teaching of Psychology*, *2*(4), 183–186.

Kinreich, S., Intrator, N., & Hendler, T. (2011). Functional cliques in the amygdala and related brain networks driven by fear assessment acquired during movie viewing. *Brain Connectivity*, *1*(6), 484–495.

Kubrak, T. (2020). Impact of films: Changes in young people's attitudes after watching a movie. *Behavioral Sciences*, *10*(5), 1–13. DOI: 10.3390/bs10050086.

Landis, J. (1988). *Coming to America* [Film]. Paramount Pictures.

Laub, D., & Auerhahn, N. C. (1993). Knowing and not knowing massive psychic trauma: Forms of traumatic memory. *International Journal of Psycho-Analysis*, *74*(2), 287–302.

Lee, M. D. (Director). (1999). *The Best Man* [Film]. Universal Pictures.

Lee, S. (Director). (1986). *She's Gotta Have It* [Film]. Island Pictures.

Lee, S. (Director). (1988). *School Daze* [Film]. Columbia Pictures.

Lee, S. (Director). (1989). *Do The Right Thing* [Film]. Universal Pictures.

Lee, S. (Director). (1990). *Mo' Better Blues* [Film]. Universal Pictures.

Lee, S. (Director). (1995). *Clockers* [Film]. Universal Pictures.

Lee, S. (Director). (2020). *Da 5 Bloods* [Film]. Netflix.

Lee, S., & Worth, M. (Directors). (1992). *Malcolm X*. Warner Bros., Warner Bros. Pictures, Largo Entertainment.

Luchies, L. B., Finkel, E. J., McNulty, J. K., & Kumashiro, M. (2010). The doormat effect: When forgiving erodes self-respect and self-concept clarity. *Journal of Personality and Social Psychology*, *98*(5), 734–749.

Magnoli, A. (Director). (1984). *Purple Rain* [Film]. Warner Bros.

Marcatto, F., & Ferrante, D. (2008). The Regret and Disappointment Scale: An instrument for assessing regret and disappointment in decision making. *Judgment and Decision Making*, *3*(1), 87–99.

Marquez, M. I. (2014). The development of the self through the "gift of the self" or the mutual recognition. *Journal for Perspectives of Economic Political and Social Integration*, *19*(1), 143–153.

Marshall, P. (Director). (1996). *The Preacher's Wife* [Film]. Buena Vista Pictures Distribution.

Bibliography 125

Marshall, T. (2015). Thurgood Marshall's stirring acceptance speech after receiving the prestigious Liberty Award on July 4, 1992. New York: NAACP Legal Defense Fund. https://www.naacpldf.org/press-release/thurgood-marshalls-stirring-acceptance-speech-after-receiving-the-prestigious-liberty-award-on-july-4-1992/.

Marshall Woods, K. (2018). *Best Psychology in Film*. Upper Marlboro, MD: PsychMinded Media.

Marshall Woods, K. (2024). Psychology and popular films. In G. J. Rich, V. K. Kumar, & F. H. Farley (Eds.), *Handbook of Media Psychology: The Science and the Practice* (pp. 131–141). Cham: Springer.

Martin, G. N. (2019). (Why) do you like scary movies? A review of the empirical research on psychological responses to horror films. *Frontiers in Psychology*, *10*, 1–22. DOI: 10.3389/fpsyg.2019.02298.

Matsoukas, M. (Director). (2019). *Queen and Slim* [Film]. Universal Pictures.

McHenry, D. (Director). (1994). *Jason's Lyric* [Film]. Gramercy Pictures, Metro-Goldwyn-Mayer.

McLaurin, V. (2012). *Stereotypes of contemporary Native American Indian characters in recent popular media* [Master's Thesis, University of Massachusetts Amherst]. ScholarWorks@UMass Amherst.

McWilliams, N. (2011). *Psychoanalytic Diagnosis* (2nd ed.). New York: The Guilford Press.

Meghie, S. (Director). (2020). *The Photograph* [Film]. Universal Pictures.

Melfi, T. (Director). (2016). *Hidden Figures* [Film]. 20th Century Fox.

Mental Health America. (2023). Black and African American communities and mental health. Alexandria, VA: Mental Health America. https://www.mhanational.org/issues/black-and-african-american-communities-and-mental-health.

Merriam-Webster. (2024a). "arrogance". https://www.merriam-webster.com/dictionary/arrogance

Merriam-Webster. (2024b). "confidence". https://www.merriam-webster.com/dictionary/confidence.

Merriam-Webster. (2024c). "entitlement". https://www.merriam-webster.com/dictionary/entitlement

Merriam-Webster. (n.d.). "liberty." https://www.merriam-webster.com/dictionary/liberty.

Metcalf, R. (2000). The truth of shame-consciousness in Freud and phenomenology. *Journal of Phenomenological Psychology*, *31*(1), 1–18.

Mihelich, J. (2001). Smoke or signals? American popular culture and the challenge to hegemonic images of American Indians in Native American film. *Wicazo Sa Review*, *16*(2), 129–137.

Miller, L. (1987). Classification of psychopathology according to a scientific (psychology and psychiatry) and an artistic (film noir) perspective. *Psychological Reports*, *61*(1), 287–299.

Mitchell, J. (2018). What did Carolyn Bryant say and when? *Mississippi Clarion Ledger*. https://www.clarionledger.com/story/news/2018/08/24/what-did-carolyn-bryant-say-and-when/1030483002/.

Moen, P., & Smith, K. R. (1986). Women at work: Commitment and behavior over the life course. *Sociological Forum*, *1*(3), 450–475.

Munoz-Dardé, V. (2016). Puzzles of regret. *Philosophy and Phenomenological Research*, *XCII*(3), 778–784.

Münsterberg, H. (1916). *The Photoplay. A Psychological Study.* New York: D. Appleton and Company.

126 Bibliography

Murphy, E. (Director). (1989). *Harlem Nights* [Film]. Paramount Pictures.

Mushonga, D. R., Rasheem, S., & Anderson, D. (2021). And still I rise: Resilience factors contributing to posttraumatic growth in African American women. *Journal of Black Psychology*, *47*(2–3), 151–176. https://doi.org/10.1177%2F0095798420979805.

Najuma Stewart, J. (2005). *Migrating to the Movies: Cinema and Black Urban Modernity*. Oakland, CA: University of California Press.

National Library of Medicine. (2014). DSM-5 diagnostic criteria for PTSD. In *Trauma-Informed Care in Behavioral Health Services*. Treatment Improvement Protocol (TIP) Series, No. 57. Rockville, MD: Center for Substance Abuse Treatment, Substance Abuse and Mental Health Services Administration. https://www.ncbi.nlm.nih.gov/books/NBK207191/box/part1_ch3.box16/.

National Museum of African American History and Culture. (2023). *Taking the stage* [Exhibition]. Washington, DC, United States.

Niemann, Y. F., Jennings, L., Rozelle, R. M., Baxter, J. C., & Sullivan, E. (1994). Use of free responses and cluster analysis to determine stereotypes of eight groups. *Personality and Social Psychology Bulletin*, *20*(4), 379–390. https://doi.org/10.1177/0146167294204005.

Niemiec, R. M. (2007). What is a positive psychology film? *PsycCritiques*, *52*(38). https://doi.org/10.1037/a0008960.

Nissim-Sabat, D. (1979). The teaching of abnormal psychology through the cinema. *Teaching of Psychology*, *6*(2), 121–123.

Olive, V. C. (2012). Sexual assault against women of color. *Journal of Student Research*, *1*(1), 1–9. https://doi.org/10.47611/jsr.v1i1.27.

Oxford Dictionaries. (2018). "conscience". https://en.oxforddictionaries.com/definition/conscience.

Oxford English Dictionary. (2023). "family". https://www.oed.com/search/dictionary/?scope=Entries&q=family.

Oxford English Dictionary. (2024a). "captivity". https://www.oed.com/search/dictionary/?scope=Entries&q=captivity.

Oxford English Dictionary. (2024b). "freedom". https://www.oed.com/search/dictionary/?scope=Entries&q=freedom.

Oxford English Dictionary. (2024c). "hostage". https://www.oed.com/search/dictionary/?scope=Entries&q=hostage.

Oxford English Dictionary. (2024d). "torture". https://www.oed.com/search/dictionary/?scope=Entries&q=torture.

Packer, W., & Hardy, R. (Directors). (2007). *Stomp the Yard* [Film]. Sony Pictures Releasing.

Paner, I. (2018). *The marginalization and stereotyping of Asians in American film* [Honors Thesis 36, Dominican University of California]. https://doi.org/10.33015/dominican.edu/2018.HONORS.ST.08.

Paz-Fuchs, A. (2016). Badges of modern slavery. *The Modern Law Review*, *79*(5), 757–785.

PBS. (1989). *Eyes on the Prize II: America at the Racial Crossroads 1965–1985. Interview with William O'Neal* [Film]. https://vimeo.com/512709094. Washington University Libraries.

Peck, R. (Director). (2016). *I Am Not Your Negro* [Film]. Magnolia Pictures.

Peele, J. (Director). (2017). *Get Out* [Film]. Universal Pictures.

Pérez-Peña, R. (2017, January 27). Women linked to 1955 Emmett Till murder tells historian her claims were false. *The New York Times*. https://www.nytimes.com/2017/01/27/us/emmett-till-lynching-carolyn-bryant-donham.html.

Perry, T. (Director). (2007). *Why Did I Get Married?* [Film]. Lionsgate.

Perry, T. (Director). (2010). *For Colored Girls* [Film]. Lionsgate.

Pianalto, M. (2011). Moral conviction. *Journal of Applied Philosophy*, *28*(4), 381–395.

Bibliography 127

Pilgrim, D. (2012). *The Jezebel stereotype* [Exhibition]. Jim Crow Museum; Ferris State University, Big Rapids, MI, United States. https://www.ferris.edu/jimcrow/jezebel/.

Pinkett Smith, J. (2023). *Worthy*. New York: RedDot Publishing.

Plantinga, C. (2011). Folk psychology for film critics and scholars. *Projections*, *5*(2), 26–50. DOI: 10.3167/proj.2011.050203.

Pollack, J., & Cooper, B. M. (Directors). *Above the Rim* [Film]. New Line Cinema.

Prince-Bythewood, G. (Director). (2000). *Love and Basketball* [Film]. New Line Cinema.

Prince-Bythewood, G. (Director). (2022). *The Woman King* [Film]. Sony Pictures Releasing.

Pruitt, S. (2021, April 15). When did African Americans actually get the right to vote? *History*. https://www.history.com/news/african-american-voting-right-15th-amendment.

Pruitt, S. (2023). Why Jesus was betrayed by Judas Iscariot. *History*. https://www.history.com/news/why-judas-betrayed-jesus#:~:text=Whatever%20his%20motives%2C%20Judas%20led,saying%20"I%20have%20sinned%20by.

Pyke, K. D. (2010). What is internalized racial oppression and why don't we study it? Acknowledging racism's hidden injuries. *Sociological Perspectives*, *53*(4), 551–572.

Raboy, M. (Director). (2002). *Friday After Next* [Film]. New Line Cinema.

Rachman, S. (2010). Betrayal: A psychological analysis. *Behaviour Research and Therapy*, *48*(3), 304–311.

Rajgopal, S. S. (2010). "The daughter of Fu Manchu": The pedagogy of deconstructing the representation of Asian women in film and fiction. *Meridians: Feminism, Race, Transnationalism*, *10*(2), 141–162. DOI: 10.2979/meridians.2010.10.2.141.

Riley, B. (Director). (2018). *Sorry to Bother You* [Film]. Annapurna Pictures (North America), Focus Features & Universal Pictures (International).

Roese, N. J., & Summerville, A. (2005). What we regret most…and why. *Personality and Social Psychology Bulletin*, *31*(9), 1273–1285.

Román, E. (2000). Who exactly is living La Vida Loca? The legal and political consequences of Latino-Latina ethnic and racial stereotypes in film and other media. *Journal of Gender, Race and Justice*, *4*(1), 37–68.

Scheff, T. J. (2000). Shame and the social bond: A sociological theory. *Sociological Theory*, *18*(1), 84–99.

Schultz, M. (Director). (1985). *Krush Groove* [Film]. Warner Bros.

Selig, W. (Director). (1898). *Something Good-Negro Kiss* [Film].

Shapiro, A. (2020, April 15). Netflix's stock is now higher than before coronavirus hit U.S.*Forbes*.https://www.forbes.com/sites/arielshapiro/2020/04/14/netflixs-stock-is-now-higher-than-before-coronavirus-hit-us-tiger-king/.

Singleton, J. (Director). (1991). *Boyz n the Hood* [Film]. Columbia Pictures.

Singleton, J. (Director). (1993). *Poetic Justice* [Film]. Columbia Pictures.

Singleton, J. (Director). (1995). *Higher Learning* [Film]. Columbia Pictures, Sony Pictures.

Singleton, J. (2019). Foreword. In D. Bogle, *Hollywood Black. The Stars, the Films, the Filmmakers* (pp. x–xi). Philadelphia, PA: Running Press.

Smith, S. G., Chen, J., Basile, K. C. Gilbert, L., K., Merrick, M. T., Patel, N., Walling, M., & Jain, A. (2017). *The National Intimate Partner and Sexual Violence Survey (NISVS): 2010–2012 State Report*. Atlanta, GA: National Center for Injury Prevention and Control, Centers for Disease Control and Prevention.

Spielberg, S. (Director). (1985). *The Color Purple* [Film]. Warner Bros.

Stone, C. (Director). (2002). *Drumline* [Film]. 20th Century Fox.

Streeter, R. (2009, October 22). Tyler Perry's amazing journey to the top. *60 Minutes, CBS News*. https://www.cbsnews.com/news/tyler-perrys-amazing-journey-to-the-top-22-10-2009/.

128 Bibliography

Sullivan, K. R. (Director). (1998). *How Stella Got Her Groove Back* [Film]. 20th Century Studios.

Tan, E. S. (2018). A psychology of the film. *Palgrave Communications*, *4*, 1–19. DOI: 10.1057/s41599-018-0111-y.

Tangney, J. P., Stuewig, J., & Martinez, A. G. (2014). Two faces of shame: The roles of shame and guilt in predicting recidivism. *Psychological Science*, *25*(3), 799–805.

Tedeschi, R. G., & Calhoun, L. G. (2004). Posttraumatic growth: Conceptual foundations and empirical evidence. *Psychological Inquiry*, *15*(1), 1–18. https://doi.org/10.1207/s15327965pli1501_01.

Tillman, G. (Director). (1997). *Soul Food* [Film]. 20th Century Studios.

Tommy, L. (Director). (2021). *Respect* [Film]. United Artists Releasing (America) & Universal Pictures (International).

Townsend, R. (Director). (1987). *Hollywood Shuffle* [Film]. The Samuel Goldwyn Company.

Townsend, R. (Director). (1991). *The Five Heartbeats* [Film]. 20th Century Studios.

Turner, J. S. (2011). Sex and the spectacle of music videos: An examination of the portrayal of race and sexuality in music videos. *Sex Roles*, *64*(3–4), 173–191.

Unger, M. (2013). Resilience, trauma, context, and culture. *Trauma, Violence, & Abuse*, *14*(3), 255–266.

Van Peebles, M. (Director). (1991). *New Jack City* [Film]. Warner Bros.

Verney, K. (2003). *African Americans and US Popular Culture*. London, UK: Routledge.

Warren-Gordon, K., & McMillan, D. M. (2022). Analysis of black female Belizean stereotypes in visual media: Jezebel, Mammy, Sapphire, and their contributions to violence against women. *Journal of International Women's Studies*, *23*(1), 248–262.

Washington, D. (Director). (2002). *Antwone Fisher* [Film]. 20th Century Fox.

Washington, D. (Director). (2016). *Fences* [Film]. Paramount Pictures.

Wayans, K. I. (Director). (1988). *I'm Gonna Git You Sucka* [Film]. MGM/UA.

West, C. M. (2008). Mammy, Jezebel, Sapphire, and their homegirls: Developing an "oppositional gaze" toward the images of African American women. In J. Chrisler, C. Golden, & P. Rozee (Eds.), *Lectures on the Psychology of Women* (4th ed., pp. 286–299). New York: McGraw-Hill.

West, C. M. (2021). Widening the lens: Expanding the research on intimate partner violence in black communities. *Journal of Aggression, Maltreatment and Trauma*, *30*(6), 749–760.

Whitaker, F. (Director). (1995). *Waiting to Exhale* [Film]. 20th Century Studios.

White, H. (1980). The value of narrativity in the representation of reality. *Critical Inquiry*, *7*(1), 5–27.

Witcher, T. (Director). (1997). *Love Jones* [Film]. New Line Cinema.

Yang, L., Xu, Z., & Luo, J. (2020). Measuring female representation and impact in films over time. *ACM/IMS Transactions on Data Science*, *1*(4), 30:1–30:14.

Yoshihara, K., Tanabe, H. C., Kawamichi, H., Koike, T., Yamazaki, M., Sudo, N., & Sadato, N. (2016). Neural correlates of fear-induced sympathetic response associated with the peripheral temperature change rate. *NeuroImage*, *134*, 522–531.

Zhao, Q., & Wichman, A. (2015). Incremental beliefs about ability ameliorate self-doubt effects. *Sage Open*, *5*(4), 1–10. DOI: 10.1177/2158244015622539.

Zillmann, D. (1991). Empathy: Affect from bearing witness to the emotions of others. In J. Bryant & D. Zillmann (Eds.), *Responding to the Screen* (pp. 135–167). Hillsdale, NJ: Erlbaum.

Zizek, S. (2019). *Cinema Guide of Pervert. Movie. Philosophy. Ideology*. Yekaterinburg, Russia: Gonzo.

Index

12 Years a Slave (2012) 90–93, 115

Above the Rim (1994) 45–49, 51–52
abuse: emotional 76–77; in home environment 22–24; physical 29; of power 114; self-protection from 68; substance 45, 47, 55
Academy of Motion Pictures Arts and Sciences 81
Academy of Motion Pictures Award *see* Oscar Award
Adams, C. 100
African American community 3, 9, 27, 36–39, 44, 64–65, 93, 114; feminist movement in 31–32; historical events in films in 81–82; Micheaux's movies about racial injustices within 17; need of army from 94; political influence of situation 33; rap and hip hop music in 20, 21, 24–25; sharing experiences of trauma 89; social issues in films 21; voices of individuals' thoughts and feelings in films 27
African American culture 24–25; in African American films 18, 20, 25, 117; appropriation by white entertainers 10; *see also* cultures of Black films
African American filmmakers 2, 4–6, 15–16, 19–20, 99, 117; acknowledging accomplishments 116; defense mechanisms 9; utilization of sublimation 10
African American men: brutal buck stereotype 30; Bobby character in *Hollywood Shuffle* 27; Bucciferro's statement on stereotypes 14; portrayed as "blackface" 15; right to vote in America 93; Shaw's experience sculpting 39

African American women: Alexander's notes about 11; Bogle's statement on *The Color Purple* film 30; feminist roles 31; intimate partner violence 65; as Mammy stereotype 12–13; stereotypes of 12, 13, 104; tropes of 104
Agojie warriors 104
Aiello, D. 33, 35
Alexander, C. S. 11, 13
Ali, M. 117
American Fiction (2023) 104–105
American Psychological Association (APA) 5, 9, 112
Andy (History of Africa Podcast) 104
Antwone Fisher (2002) 68, 76–78
The Autobiography of Malcolm X (Haley and Shabazz) 64

"badges of slavery" 82
Baggett, S. 119
Baldwin, J. 19, 85–86
Bassett, A. 62, 85
Bell, V. 31
Benedetti, F. 5
Bennett, L. J. 92
Berry, H. 59, 117
The Best Man (1991) 56
The Best Man (1999) 116
The Best Man Holiday, (2013) 56
The Best Man: The Final Chapter (2022) 56
Best Psychology in Film (Woods) 6, 19, 70, 81–82
betrayal, acts of 48, 63, 74, 84, 107
Bird, H. 83
The Birth of a Nation (1915) 15
"blackface" 15
Black Lives Matter 112
"Black on Black Crime" (song by Stanley Clarke band) 114

130 Index

Black Panther (2018) 84–85
Black Panther Party 106–107
Blaxploitation cinema/films 18, 21
The Blood of Emmett Till (Tyson) 112
body of evidence 15
Bogle, D. 30
Boomerang (1992) 57, 58–60
Boseman, C. 84
Boyz N The Hood (1991) 44–46, 50–51, 92, 114, 115
Braugher, A. 40
Brown, C. 75
Brown, S, K. 105
Brown Sugar (2002) 116
Bryant Donham, C. 112
Bryant, R. 112
Bucciferro, C. 4, 14
Burr, C. 25

Caesar, A. 21, 30
Cameron, M. 75
Cannon, N. 70
captivity 95–96; and 1967 Detroit riots 95; emotional 29; as hostage 115; in *If Beale Street Could Talk* film 85; indefinite 108; and slavery 82, 91–92; of spousal abusive relationships 65
Carroll, D. 18
Carter, T. W. 119
cartoons 11
Carveth, D. 88
Chambers, M. 119
Charles, R. 78–79
Cinematic Imprints program 5
cinematography 2, 64
Clarke, S. 114
Clockers (1995) 45–47, 50
cognitive disorganization 90
cognitive distress 29
The Color Purple (1988) 28–30, 115
Colors (1988) 30–31
comedy 3, 18, 21, 44; *Clockers* 50; *Hollywood Shuffle* 20, 27; Tyler Perry's movies 67
Coming to America (1988) 31–32
Community Resources Against Street Hoodlums (C. R. A. S. H.) 30
conscience 59, 87–89
Cooper, B. M. 115
Cooper, C. 95
Covid-19 impact in film production 99–100; *see also* independent (indie) films
cultural violence 29

cultures of Black films 20–21, 37; comedy in 27; death in 100–101; fraternities and sororities in 75–76; micro-cultures in universities 37; race movies representing 16; rap and hip hop 20, 21, 24–25; *see also* African American culture
Currie, G. 3

Da 5 Bloods (2020) 100–101
Dalton, P. S. 109
dance preferences 6, 21, 24, 38, 43, 65, 75
David, E. J. R. 22
Davis, O. 33
Davis, S. Jr. 42
Davis, V. 103, 117
Day, M. 24
Dead Presidents (1995) 45–47
death instinct 44–45, 51, 59, 86
Dee, R. 33
defense mechanism 5, 9, 45, 78, 108, 114, 115; in *Love and Basketball* 69–70, 116; in *She's Gotta Have It* 20, 25–26
depression 3, 58, 110–111
Deskins, S. 119
Detroit (2017) 95–96, 114
Diagnostic and Statistical Manual of Mental Disorders, Fifth Edition, Text Revision (DSM-V-TR) 46
Diggs, T. 63
displacement 5, 21
documentaries 8, 108
domestic violence 29; *Jason's Lyric* and 48; *Purple Rain* and 22–24; *What's Love Got to Do With It* and 45, 65–66
Domingo, C. 85
Dorsey, M. 47
Do the Right Thing (1989) 20, 32–34
Douglas, S. 42, 53
Douglass, F. 82, 84
Dreamettes in *Dreamgirls* 74
Dreamgirls (2006) 73–75
Drumline (2002) 70–71
DSM-V-TR *see* Diagnostic and Statistical Manual of Mental Disorders, Fifth Edition, Text Revision
Duncan, L. 33
Duvall, R. 30
DuVernay, A. 93, 117

Edmund, J. P. 55
Edson, R. 33
ego 58–60, 87
The Ego and the Id (Freud) 87

Ejiofor, C. 90
emotional/emotion(s) 41, 89; captivity 29; conflict 73; consequences 46, 110; death 86; disorganization 90; distress 5, 29, 45–46; fortitude 30, 93; functioning 100; grievances 110; harshness 101; home 70; investment 103; needs 102; positive 50; safety 77; self 58; terror 114
Epps, O. 52, 60, 69
escapism 10, 78
Esposito, G. 33, 37
Evans, A. 22

family concept films 54–57; *see also* domestic violence
fashion 21, 24, 25, 90
fear 11, 53, 54, 76, 89, 109; in *King Richard* 108
feature films 8, 67, 81
feminist movement 31
Fences (2016) 70, 81–82
filmmakers *see* African American filmmakers
Fishburne, L. 37
The Five Heartbeats (1991) 54–55
folk psychology 6
For Colored Girls (2010) 12, 81
Fox, V. A. 47–48, 56
Foxx, J. 74, 78
freedom concept films 20, 81–82; *Black Panther* 84–85; *Fences* 70, 81–82; *Get Out* 82–84; *Glory* 39–40; *If Beale Street Could Talk* 85–87; *Moonlight* 82; *Queen and Slim* 89–90; *Sorry to Bother You* 87–89; *see also* independent (indie) films
Freeman, M. 40, 41, 117
free will 83, 114, 115
Freud, S.: death instinct 45; drive theory 110; *The Ego and the Id* 87; personality theory 58; Pleasure Principle 59; uncanny 60
Fuller, C. 21

Gasque, P. 119
Get Out (2017) 82–84
Gillum, T. L. 13
Givens, R. 59
Glory (1989) 32, 36, 39–40
Glover, D. 88
Glover, S. 42
Godos, H. 83
Goff, P. A. 112

Goldberg, W. 63
Gooden, W. E. 13
Gooding, C., Jr. 117
The Great Debaters (2007) 68, 79–80, 92
Greene, B. 12
grief: in *12 Years a Slave* 92; in *Above the Rim* 51; in *Dreamgirls* 74; entertaining public during 11; in *Higher Learning* 60–61; in *Malcolm X* 64; in *Poetic Justice* 49, 51; in *Stomp the Yard* 76; in *The Photograph* 101; and "What ifs" 57
Grier, D. A. 59
Grier, P. 18
Guy, J. 35

Haley, A. 64
Hammond, B. 56
Hampton, F. 106, 107
Hampton, R. 13
Harlem Nights (1989) 32, 34–36
HBCU *see* Historically Black College and University
Headley, S. 32
Hicks, T. R. 25
Hidden Figures (2016) 81, 95
Higher Learning (1995) 44, 60–61
Hines, G. 42, 43
Hines II, D. A. 35
hip hop culture 20, 21, 24–25
Historically Black College and University (HBCU) 38, 79
historical trauma 29
Hollywood Shuffle (1987) 20, 27
hopelessness 44, 53, 54, 76, 89, 92
Horne, L. 17, 117
horror 2, 3; *12 Years a Slave* 90–93, 115; *Antwone Fisher* 76; Jordan Peele's contribution 84
Houston, W. 55
How Stella Got Her Groove Back (1998) 57, 62–63
Hudson, J. 13, 74
human psyche 58
humor 21, 50, 61, 68, 105
hurt 12, 56, 59, 61, 70, 73
Hustle and Flow (2005) 72–73

Ice-T 115
id 58–60, 87
If Beale Street Could Talk (2018) 85–87
independent (indie) films 28–29, 99–100; *American Fiction* 104–105; *Da 5 Bloods* 100–101; legacy films 106–112; *The*

Photograph 101–102; *The Woman King* 102–104
institutional violence 29
internalized racism 22
interpersonal dynamics 32
intimate partner violence (IPV) 29, 65; *see also* domestic violence
intrusive symptomatology 48

Jackson, J. 47
Jackson, M. 112
Jackson, S. 39
James, S. 85
Jason's Lyric (1994) 45–49, 53
Jefferson, C. 117
Jenkins, B. 117
Jezebel stereotype 12–13
Jim Crow laws 79
Johnson, G. P. 16
Johnson, L. B. 94
Johnson, N. M. 16
Johns, T. C. 25
Jones, J. E. 32
Jordan, M. B. 85
Judas and the Black Messiah (2021) 106–108
Juice (1992) 45–47, 52

Kaluuya, D. 82, 89, 117
Keitel, H. 47
Kelly, J. F. 12
Kennedy, J. 40
Kimble Wrye, H. 31
King, C. S. 94
King, M. L., Jr. 18, 33, 93–95
King Richard (2021) 108–109
Kinreich, S. 5
Klein, R. 47, 50
Knowles, B. 74
Kotero, A. 23
Krush Groove (1985) 24–25
Ku Klux Klan 15, 64

Larry, J. L. 96
Latham, S. 69
Latinx community 14
Laudry, L. 2
Layne, K. 85
Lean on Me (1989) 40–42
learning 41–42; children's behaviors 87; with film 3–5; higher 38; *Higher Learning* 44, 60–61
Lee, J. 33, 57

Lee, M. D. 56
Lee, S. 20, 25–26, 32–33, 36–37, 44, 57
legacy films 63–64, 68–69, 81, 106; *Till* 93, 111–112, 115; *12 Years a Slave* 90–93, 115; *Antwone Fisher* 76–78; *Detroit* 95–96, 114; *Glory* 39–40; *Great Debaters* 79–80; *Hidden Figures* 81, 95; *Judas and the Black Messiah* 106–108; *King Richard* 108–109; *Lean on Me* 40–42; *Malcolm X* 64–65; *Marshall* 96–98; *Ray* 78–79; *Respect* 109–111; *School Daze* 36–39; *Selma* 93–95; *Tap* 42–43; *What's Love Got to Do With It* 45, 65–66
Leon 47, 54
Lerner, M. 35
Lewis, J. 55
Lewis, N. 100
libidinal drive 44, 59, 65
Lincoln Motion Pictures Company 16
Lindo, D. 100
Lloyd, T. H. 119
logical self 58
Long, N. 56
Look Magazine 112
Love and Basketball (2000) 69–70, 116
love concept films 57–63
Love Jones (1997) 61–62, 116
love triangles 61
Lowe, H. 92
Luchies, L. B. 108
Ludacris 72
Luke, D. 76

Madea films 67–68
Majors, J. 100
Malcolm X (1992) 64–65
Mammy stereotype 12–13
Manning, T. 73
Marshall (2017) 96–98
Marshall, T. 96–97
Maslow's Hierarchy of Needs 29–30
Maxson, T. 70
Mazilli, L. 47, 50
Mbedu, T. 103
McDaniel, H. 17, 117
Meadows, R. 38
Menace II Society (1993) 45–47, 49, 52, 115
mental health: Americans engagement with stigma in relation to 3; demise resulting in suicide 22; narrative in *Malcolm X* film 64; stigma 3

Index

Micheaux, O. 16–18
micro-cultures 37
Milam, J. W. 112
Mitchell, R. 106
Mo' Better Blues (1990) 57–58
Moen, P. 103
Moonlight (2016) 81–82
Münsterberg, H. 2, 10
Murphy, E. 31, 35, 59, 74
Muse, C. 17
music 2, 21, 110; *Drumline* 70–71;
    The Five Heartbeats 54–55; Jezebel
    stereotype in 13; *Krush Groove* 24–25;
    What's Love Got to Do With It 5, 65–66;
    see also hip hop culture

NAACP *see* National Association for the
    Advancement of Colored People
narrative fiction 5–6
National Association for the Advancement
    of Colored People (NAACP) 30, 96–97
National Intimate Partner and Sexual
    Violence Survey (NISVS) 65
Nation of Islam 64
Native Americans 14–15
Nelson, J. A. 115
Nelson, N. 77
Netflix 99
New Jack City (1991) 115
Nicholas, H. 42
Nichols, N. 119
Niemann, Y. F. 13
nightmares 48, 49
Nope (2022) 84
Nunn, B. 33

Oduye, A. 92
Oliver, W. 13
Oscar Award 17
Out of the Shadows (Bird) 83

Paner, I. 14
Parker, P. J. 72
Payne, A. 47, 115
Paz-Fuchs, A. 82–83
Peebles, M V. 115
Peele, J. 82, 84
Penn, S. 30
Perdue, A. 119
Pérez-Peña, R. 112
Perez, R. 33
Perry, T. 12, 67–68

personality theory (Freud) 58
Peters, C. 100
Phifer, M. 47
The Photograph (2020) 101–102, 116
The Photoplay: A Psychological Study
    (Münsterberg) 2
Plantinga, C. 6, 19
Pleasure Principle 59
Poetic Justice (1993) 44–47, 49, 51
Poitier, S. 17–18, 117
Pollard, A. 95
post-traumatic growth 66
post-traumatic stress disorder (PTSD) 46,
    53, 100–101
"Powercaller" 88
The Preacher's Wife (1996) 55–56
Price, R. 47
Prior, R. 35
psychodynamic theory 1, 18–19, 101, 119
psychological accuracy 1, 104
psychological dynamics 4, 102, 115
psychopathology theory 4
Purple Rain (1984) 22–24
Pyke, K. D. 22

Queen and Slim (2019) 89–90

Rachman, S. 107
Rae, I. 100
Rapaport, M. 60
rape cases 13, 29, 65, 85
Rawlins, J. 40
Ray (2004) 68, 78–79
Regeneration:Black Cinema 1898–1971
    exhibit 119
regret narrative 69–70, 108
Respect (2021) 109–111
Riley, B. 87
Roberts, L. 71
Rock, C. 115
Roese, N. J. 69–70
Rollins, H. E., Jr. 21
Román, E. 14
Ross, D. 18
Ruth, R. 119

sadness 5, 12, 53, 70, 89; *Above the Rim*
    51; *Higher Learning* 60–61; *Waiting to*
    Exhale 55
Sapphire stereotype 12, 72
Saunders, J. 119
School Daze (1988) 36–39

134 Index

Searles, T. 40
self-actualization 30
self-concept 11, 13, 22, 31, 79
self-esteem 11, 13, 22, 34
self-worth 38, 73
Selma (2014) 93–95
Set It Off (1996) 45–48, 51
Sex and the City (2008) 13
Shabazz, A. 64
Shakur, T. 52
shame, feeling of 40, 79–80, 103, 108
Shapiro, A. 99
Sharts, J. 40
Shaw, R. G. 39
She's Gotta Have It (1986) 20, 25–26
Short, C. 75
"the silent era" 11, 15
Simmons, R. 24
Sims, H. S. 42
Sinclair, M. 32
Singleton, J. 44
slavery/enslavements: and *12 Years a Slave*
   90–93, 115; badges of 82; in *Get Out*
   84; and Jezebel stereotype 12–13; and
   Mammy stereotype 12–13; modern 82,
   83; physical and emotional enslavements
   29; and transatlantic slave trade 103, 104
Slyde, J. 42
Smith, A. 96
Smith, J. P. 44
Smith, J. T. 89
Smith, K. R. 103
Smith, R. G. 33
Smith, W. 108
Snipes, W. 58, 115
A Soldier's Story (1984) 21–22
"sophisticated self-consciousness" 79
sorrow 12, 30, 53, 55, 63, 70
Sorry to Bother You (2018) 87–89
Soul Food (1997) 54, 56
space, race films 15–16
Stanfield, L. 83, 87, 100, 106
stereotypes 17, 27, 31, 54, 103; of Black
   women 104; brutal buck 30; internalized
   53; Jezebel stereotype 12–13; Mammy
   stereotype 12–13; negative 10, 14,
   53, 84; positive 14; racial 21, 22, 68;
   Sapphire stereotype 12, 72; tropes 14
stigma 2, 3
Stomp the Yard (2007) 75–76
structural violence 29
sublimation 9–10, 115

substance use 42, 49, 65, 74, 78
Summerville, A. 69–70
superego 58–59, 87, 88, 89
Swanson, K. 60

Taking the Stage (exhibition) 119
Tap (1989) 42–43
Temple, F. 95
Terrell, J. C. 25
Thompson, D. 119
Till (2022) 93, 111–112, 115
Till, E. 111–112
Till-Mobley, M. 111
Townsend, R. 20, 27, 54
tragedy in Black films 45, 110
trauma 13, 29, 38, 45–54, 64–66, 76–78,
   89–92, 95; emotional 24; healing/
   recovery process from 43, 96;
   intergenerational 23
tripartite model 87
tropes 13, 14, 18, 104; auditory tropes in
   horror 2; racial 11–12, 116
Tucker, C. 47
Turner, I. 65
Turner, S. D. 109–110
Turner, T. 47, 65–66
Turturro, J. 33, 47
Tyson, C. 18
Tyson, T. B. 112

Unger, M. 77
Us (2019) 84

Vance, C. B. 55, 100
Verney, K. 9
visceral vulnerability 114
visual art 21

Waiting to Exhale (1995) 54, 55
Wakanda Forever (2022) 85
Walker, A. 28, 30
Warren, S. 78
Washington Baltimore Center for
   Psychoanalysis 4
Washington, D. 40, 56, 57, 77, 79, 117
Wells, T. 55
West, C. M. 11–12, 65
"What ifs" 57
What's Love Got to Do With It (1993) 45,
   65–66
Whitaker, D. 80
Whitaker, F. 79

Whitford, B. 82
Whitlock, I., Jr. 100
Why Did I Get Married? (Perry) 12
Williams, A. 82–83
Williams, C. 57
Williams, R. R. 117
Williams, V. 56
The Woman King (2022) 102–104
The Wood (1999) 56

Woodbine, B. 49
Worthy (Smith) 44
Wright, J. 105
Wright, L. 85
Wright, M. 55
Wright, T. L. 115
Writers Guild of America's strike 99

Yoshihara, K. 5

Milton Keynes UK
Ingram Content Group UK Ltd.
UKHW031330071224
451979UK00005B/56